SCHOLASTIC

100 Task Cards
Informational Text

Reproducible Mini-Passages With Key Questions to Boost Reading Comprehension Skills

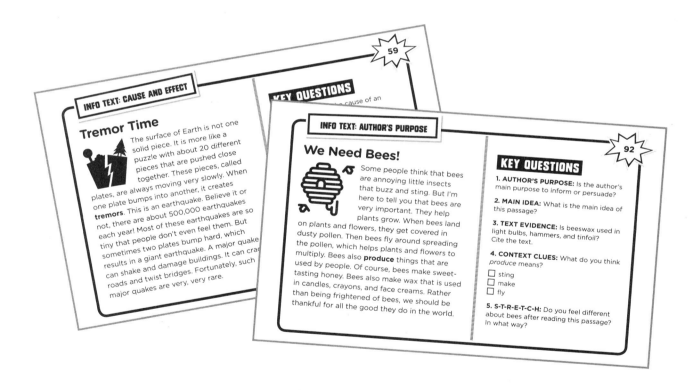

INFO TEXT: CAUSE AND EFFECT

Tremor Time

The surface of Earth is not one solid piece. It is more like a puzzle with about 20 different pieces that are pushed close together. These pieces, called plates, are always moving very slowly. When one plate bumps into another, it creates **tremors**. This is an earthquake. Believe it or not, there are about 500,000 earthquakes each year! Most of these earthquakes are so tiny that people don't even feel them. But sometimes two plates bump hard, which results in a giant earthquake. A major quake can shake and damage buildings. It can crack roads and twist bridges. Fortunately, such major quakes are very, very rare.

INFO TEXT: AUTHOR'S PURPOSE

We Need Bees!

Some people think that bees are annoying little insects that buzz and sting. But I'm here to tell you that bees are very important. They help plants grow. When bees land on plants and flowers, they get covered in dusty pollen. Then bees fly around spreading the pollen, which helps plants and flowers to multiply. Bees also **produce** things that are used by people. Of course, bees make sweet-tasting honey. Bees also make wax that is used in candles, crayons, and face creams. Rather than being frightened of bees, we should be thankful for all the good they do in the world.

KEY QUESTIONS

1. AUTHOR'S PURPOSE: Is the author's main purpose to inform or persuade?

2. MAIN IDEA: What is the main idea of this passage?

3. TEXT EVIDENCE: Is beeswax used in light bulbs, hammers, and tinfoil? Cite the text.

4. CONTEXT CLUES: What do you think produce means?

☐ sting
☐ make
☐ fly

5. S-T-R-E-T-C-H: Do you feel different about bees after reading this passage? In what way?

New York • Toronto • London • Auckland • Sydney
Mexico City • New Delhi • Hong Kong • Buenos Aires

Passages written by Carol Ghiglieri and Justin Martin
Cover design by Tannaz Fassihi
Cover photo © Eric Audras/PhotoAlto/Getty Images.
Interior design by Grafica, Inc.
Interior illustrations by The Noun Project

ISBN: 978-1-338-11299-3

Scholastic Inc., 557 Broadway, New York, NY 10012
Copyright © 2017 by Scholastic Inc.
All rights reserved.
Printed in the U.S.A.
Published by Scholastic Inc.
First printing, January 2017.

7 8 9 10   40   25 24 23 22 21 20 19

CONTENTS

INTRODUCTION

Welcome to *100 Task Cards: Informational Text!*

The vast majority of what we read is nonfiction: newspaper articles, biographies, sports stories, science books, business memos, blogs, history titles, editorials, health care information, instruction manuals, textbooks, advertisements, websites, memoirs, persuasive essays, magazine features, and more.

But navigating this diverse array of informational texts can be a daunting task—especially for kids! The truth is some of them are not achieving "deep comprehension" because they've yet to master core nonfiction reading skills, including the ability to identify the main idea of an article, summarize a news story, compare and contrast elements within a text, separate facts from opinions, understand an author's purpose, or accrue new vocabulary words via context clues. Plus, with the rigorous literacy standards currently in place, that means our students may be failing on the standardized tests, too.

But don't despair. This practical resource is here to help students vastly improve their nonfiction comprehension skills—and meet your challenging state standards—in just minutes a day! The 100 task cards in this book offer motivating mini-passages with key questions related to:

- **Main Idea and Details**
- **Sequence of Events**
- **Summarizing**
- **Comparing and Contrasting**
- **Problem and Solution**
- **Cause and Effect**
- **Fact and Opinion**
- **Debate**
- **Description**
- **Author's Purpose**

The cards are designed for instant use—just photocopy, cut them apart, and they're good to go. The cards are also designed for flexible use. They're perfect for seatwork, centers, or meaningful homework. They're great for independent practice or work with partners, small groups, and even the whole class.

The questions on the cards, which can be responded to orally or in writing, will help students hone critical comprehension skills they'll rely on for a lifetime. And here's more good news: Because the mini-passages were written by professional authors with a gift for engaging young readers, kids will absolutely *love* them!

So what are you waiting for? Read on for tips that will help your students grow into confident, fluent, "deep" readers—quickly and painlessly. And don't forget to look for the other great books in this series, including *100 Task Cards: Literary Text* and *100 Task Cards: Text Evidence*. The kids in your class will thank you.

TEACHING TIPS

About the 100 Informational Text Task Cards

This book contains 100 cards, each presenting an informational mini-passage. The texts vary by topic, form, purpose, and tone in an effort to give students a rich variety of reading material that correlates with current state standards. (For a list of the standards these cards address, see page 8.) Each card presents five key questions, including one related to context clues. This special feature is intended to boost your students' abilities to glean the meaning of unfamiliar words they encounter in all texts.

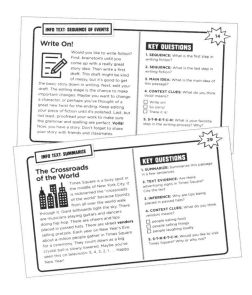

The cards address the following ten categories: main idea and details, sequencing, summarizing, comparing and contrasting, problem and solution, cause and effect, fact and opinion, debate, description, and author's purpose. You will find the target skill in the upper left-hand corner of each card. The mini-passages can be used in any order you choose. However, if you are teaching a certain topic or wish to help students hone a particular skill—such as understanding main idea and details—you can simply assign one or more cards from that category.

SAMPLE CARD: Here's a quick tour of a task card.

FOCUS TOPIC

MINI-PASSAGE (approximately 100 words)

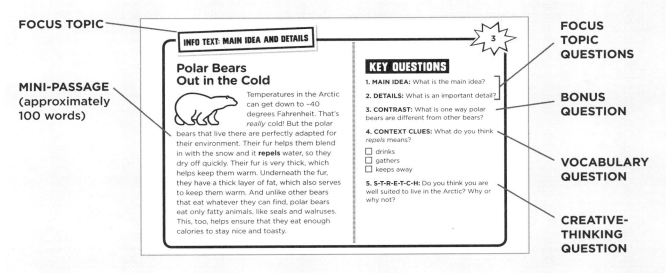

FOCUS TOPIC QUESTIONS

BONUS QUESTION

VOCABULARY QUESTION

CREATIVE-THINKING QUESTION

About the 14 Comprehension Helper Cards

To scaffold student learning, we've provided 14 Comprehension Helper Cards. (See pages 9–15.) These "bonus" cards, on topics ranging from main idea and details to fact and opinion, are intended to provide age-perfect background information that will help students respond knowledgeably to the five questions on the task cards. We suggest you photocopy a set for each student to have at the ready.

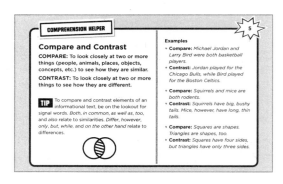

About the Answer Key

We've also included a complete answer key. (See pages 67–80.) In the key, we've provided sample responses to the questions on all 100 cards. Please note that student answers will vary. Because many of the questions are open-ended and no two minds work exactly alike, we encourage you to accept—and applaud—all reasonable answers.

MAKING THE TASK CARDS

The task cards are easy to make. Just photocopy the pages and cut along the dashed lines.

- **Tip #1:** For sturdier cards, photocopy the pages on card stock and/or laminate them.

- **Tip #2:** To make the cards extra appealing, use different colors of paper or card stock for each category of card.

- **Tip #3:** To store the cards, use a plastic lunch bag or a recipe box. Or, hole punch the corner of each card and place on a key ring.

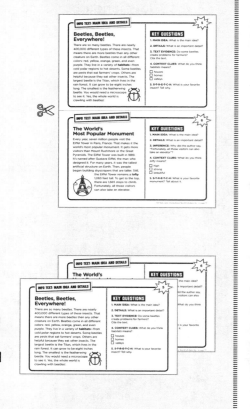

First-Time Teaching Routine

Any text will become accessible to students who bring strong reading strategies to the table. Here's an easy routine for introducing the task cards to your students for the very first time.

1. Display an enlarged version of the task card using an interactive whiteboard, document camera, or overhead projector.

2. Cover the mini-passage and display just the title. Read it aloud and invite students to predict what the nonfiction article will be about.

3. Read the mini-passage aloud, slowly and clearly.

4. Boost fluency by inviting a student volunteer to read the mini-passage again using his or her best "performance" voice.

5. Discuss the mini-passage. Encourage students to comment and connect it to other texts as well as to their own lives.

6. Call attention to the five key questions to the right of the mini-passage.

7. Challenge students to respond thoughtfully to each question.
   TIP: Use a highlighter to mark clues to the answers within the text.

8. Number and record each answer on a chart pad. Model using complete sentences with proper spelling and punctuation.

9. Build comprehension by working with students to craft a brand-new question related to the text. Then, answer it.

10. Give your class a round of applause for successfully completing a task card. Now they're ready to tackle the cards independently.

INTEGRATING THE TASK CARDS INTO THE CLASSROOM

The task cards can be used in many ways. Here are ten quick ideas to maximize learning:

- Challenge students to complete one task card every morning.

- Invite partners to read the task cards together and respond in writing.

- Invite small groups to read, discuss, and respond to the task cards orally.

- Place the task cards in a learning center for students to enjoy independently.

- Carve out time to do a task card with the whole class a few times a week.

- Encourage individual students to build fluency by reading a task card aloud to the class. They can then solicit from fellow students answers to the questions.

- Laminate the task cards and place them in a recipe box for students to do after they've completed the rest of their work.

- Send the task cards home for students to complete with or without parental help.

- Provide students with designated notebooks for recording the answers to all of the task cards.

- Create a class chart, telling students to make a check mark each time they complete a task card. The first student to reach 100 wins a prize!

CONNECTION TO THE INFORMATIONAL TEXT STANDARDS

The lessons in this book support the College and Career Readiness Anchor Standards for Reading in Grades K–12. These broad standards, which serve as the basis for many state standards, were developed to establish rigorous educational expectations with the goal of providing students nationwide with a quality education that prepares them for college and careers.

Key Ideas and Details

- Refer to details and examples in a text when explaining what the text says explicitly and when drawing inferences from the text.
- Determine the main idea of a text and explain how it is supported by key details; summarize the text.
- Explain events, procedures, ideas, or concepts in a historical, scientific, or technical text, including what happened and why, based on specific information in the text.
- Quote accurately from a text when explaining what the text says explicitly and when drawing inferences from the text.
- Cite textual evidence to support analysis of what the text says explicitly as well as inferences drawn from the text.

Craft and Structure

- Determine the meaning of general academic and domain-specific words or phrases in a text relevant to an age-appropriate topic or subject area.
- Describe the overall structure (e.g., chronology, comparison, cause/effect, problem/solution) of events, ideas, concepts, or information in a text or part of a text.

Integration of Knowledge and Ideas

- Explain how an author uses reasons and evidence to support particular points in a text.
- Analyze how a particular sentence, paragraph, chapter, or section fits into the overall structure of a text and contributes to the development of the ideas.
- Determine an author's point of view or purpose in a text and explain how it is conveyed in the text.
- Trace and evaluate the argument and specific claims in a text, distinguishing claims that are supported by reasons and evidence from claims that are not.

Source: © Copyright 2010 National Governors Association Center for Best Practices and Council of Chief State School Officers. All rights reserved.

Informational Text

Text that provides facts and information to readers. Synonym: Nonfiction.

TIP *Before reading,* think about what you already know about the topic. Also think about questions you'd like answered in the text. *During reading,* take your time. Try to determine the main idea and key details. *After reading,* reflect on what you just read. Reread any confusing parts. Talk about the text with a classmate.

Examples

- *news stories*
- *textbooks*
- *business memos*
- *magazine articles*
- *advertisements*
- *personal essays*
- *humor essays*
- *nonfiction books*
- *health-care pamphlets*
- *assembly instructions*
- *campaign information*
- *biographies*
- *sports articles*
- *history titles*
- *editorials*
- *recipes*
- *opinion pieces*
- *memoirs*

Main Idea and Details

MAIN IDEA: The big idea, or main point, of a text. The main idea answers this question: *What* is the piece of writing about?

DETAILS: Facts, statements, descriptions, and other information that tell more about the main idea.

TIP Think of the main idea as a big umbrella that "covers" all the smaller details. The main idea of an informational text is often stated as a topic sentence, which can appear anywhere in the text. Be on the lookout for it!

Examples

- **Main Idea:** *Wolves are fascinating mammals.*
- **Detail:** *Wolves live in packs.*

- **Main Idea:** *New York City is a large, diverse city.*
- **Detail:** *Eight million people live in New York City.*

- **Main Idea:** *There are eight planets in our solar system.*
- **Detail:** *The largest planet is Jupiter.*

- **Main Idea:** *Abraham Lincoln was a great president.*
- **Detail:** *Lincoln wrote the Gettysburg Address.*

Sequence of Events

EVENTS: Important things that happen in a text.

SEQUENCE: The order in which those things happen.

TIP When reading informational text, it is very important to understand the sequence of events. Signal words provide clues that help clarify the order of events. Examples include *first, second, then, next, before, after that, later, last,* and *finally,* as well as specific dates and times.

Example

• **Sequence of events for making a pizza:** *First, you roll out the dough. Second, you ladle on the tomato sauce. Then, you sprinkle on the cheese. Next, you put on the pepperoni. After that, you put on the mushrooms. Last, you bake it in the oven.*

Summarize

Creating a brief statement about a text using only the most important details.

TIP When writing a summary, think about how to retell the key ideas of a passage in your own words. Challenge yourself to be short and clear *and* to leave out all the unimportant details.

Example

• **Sample Text:** *Cats make excellent pets. From Nepal to New York—cats are the world's favorite pet! Cats are mammals like bears and bats. The difference is that cats are gentle and enjoy living with people. There are more than 70 breeds of cats. Cats are fairly easy to care for. They don't need to be walked several times a day like dogs. Plus, they love to sleep. In fact, some cats sleep up to 20 hours a day.*

• **Summary of Text:** *Cats make excellent pets for people all over the world. There are more than 70 different breeds of this gentle mammal. Cats are easy to care for.*

Compare and Contrast

COMPARE: To look closely at two or more things (people, animals, places, objects, concepts, etc.) to see how they are similar.

CONTRAST: To look closely at two or more things to see how they are different.

TIP To compare and contrast elements of an informational text, be on the lookout for signal words. *Both*, *in common*, *as well as*, *too*, and *also* relate to similarities. *Differ*, *however*, *only*, *but*, *while*, and *on the other hand* relate to differences.

Examples

- **Compare:** *Michael Jordan and Larry Bird were both basketball players.*
- **Contrast:** *Jordan played for the Chicago Bulls, while Bird played for the Boston Celtics.*

- **Compare:** *Squirrels and mice are both rodents.*
- **Contrast:** *Squirrels have big, bushy tails. Mice, however, have long, thin tails.*

- **Compare:** *Squares are shapes. Triangles are shapes, too.*
- **Contrast:** *Squares have four sides, but triangles have only three sides.*

Problem and Solution

PROBLEM: A difficulty that needs fixing.

SOLUTION: How that difficulty gets repaired or resolved.

TIP Some nonfiction texts present a challenging situation to engage readers, then offer a solution to the problem. Words that signal a problem include *question, obstacle, unfortunately, dilemma, issue, puzzle, need,* and *trouble.* Words that signal a solution include *answer, result, one reason, solve, improve, prevent, invent, fix, correct,* and *remedy.*

Examples

- **Problem:** *Children are getting sick with polio.*
- **Solution:** *A doctor solves the problem by developing a vaccine.*

- **Problem:** *People need to move heavy things.*
- **Solution:** *People invent the wheel.*

- **Problem:** *Unfortunately, elephants have become an endangered species in Africa.*
- **Solution:** *African countries pass laws that prohibit the hunting of elephants, which protects them from becoming extinct.*

COMPREHENSION HELPER

Cause and Effect

CAUSE: The action or reason something happens.

EFFECT: The result or outcome of that action.

TIP Some informational texts show a relationship between something that happens and its outcome. Words that signal cause and effect include *due to, as a result, since, therefore, because of, caused, led, for this reason, so that, in order to,* and *led to.*

Examples

- **Cause:** *Gold is discovered in California.*
- **Effect:** *For this reason, thousands move to California to become rich.*

- **Cause:** *Lightning strikes a house.*
- **Effect:** *Because of the lightning, a house catches on fire.*

- **Cause:** *The U.S. government passes laws to protect spotted owls.*
- **Effect:** *As a result, the spotted owl population increases.*

- **Cause:** *The* Titanic *crashes into an iceberg.*
- **Effect:** *This caused the* Titanic *to sink.*

COMPREHENSION HELPER

Fact and Opinion

FACT: A piece of information that is true. Facts don't vary.

OPINION: A personal belief or feeling. Opinions do vary.

TIP Some nonfiction texts include facts, opinions, or both. Words that signal facts include *proof, know, data, indicate, discovered,* and *research shows.* Words that signal opinions include *believe, think, wish, expect, disagree, probably, seems to, hope, viewpoint,* and *feel.*

Examples

- **Fact:** *I know dolphins are mammals.*
- **Opinion:** *I think dolphins are cute.*

- **Fact:** *My book states that George Washington was the first U.S. president.*
- **Opinion:** *The author believes George Washington was the very best president.*

- **Fact:** *Scientists have discovered more than two million different insects.*
- **Opinion:** *I wish insects would stay far away!*

Debate

A discussion between two (or more) sides with different views.

TIP Some informational texts include debates, which present two or more sides of an issue. Often, the purpose of this type of text is to convince you that the author's viewpoint is the correct one. But, as the reader, you have the option to agree or disagree.

Examples

- *Do you think school uniforms are good or bad?*
- *Should animals be placed in zoos— yes or no?*
- *Is it better to vacation near mountains or the ocean?*
- *Washington or Lincoln: Who was the best U.S. president?*
- *Should astronauts visit Mars? Why or why not?*
- *Should colleges be free or should students pay to attend them?*
- *Are printed books better than e-books?*
- *Which pet is the very best—a dog, a cat, or a fish?*

Description

When words are used to create a "picture" in the mind.

TIP Good descriptions activate the senses and often include details about how something looks, sounds, smells, tastes, or feels. Descriptions help readers understand and explore a topic more deeply. To "view" a description, close your eyes after reading it and try to make a picture in your mind's eye.

Examples

- *The tiny ladybug was ruby red with little, black spots.*
- *The perfume smelled like roses mixed with red licorice.*
- *The sound of her trumpet playing reminded me of a braying donkey.*
- *A new variety of grapes tastes exactly like sweet, sugary cotton candy.*
- *A shark's skin feels as rough as sandpaper.*

COMPREHENSION HELPER

Author's Purpose

The *reason* the author chose to write a text. Authors may write with more than one purpose in mind.

TIP Every author has goals in mind when he or she writes. To figure out an author's purpose, read the text closely and ask yourself these questions: *Is the author trying to tell me something?* (Inform) *Is the author trying to convince me of something?* (Persuade) *Is the author trying to amuse me?* (Entertain) Also ask: *Is the author trying to do just one of these things or more?*

Examples

- **Writing to Inform** *(tell, explain, describe, teach, update)*
- **Writing to Persuade** *(convince, advise, influence, sway, talk you into)*
- **Writing to Entertain** *(please, inspire, move, amuse)*

COMPREHENSION HELPER

Text Evidence

Exact words, phrases, and sentences in a text that provide information, answer a question, or support a claim.

TIP When citing text in a story, frame your text evidence with a sentence stem, such as: *According to the text*. Follow that with a comma or colon (, or :). Then place the **exact words** from the text in quotation marks. (See examples on the right.)

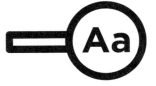

Examples

- *According to the text, "Grizzly bears usually emerge from hibernation in early spring."*
- *The main idea in this text is, "Smoking is very bad for your health for a number of reasons."*
- *The author states: "Medieval castles ranged from simple wood structures to massive stone compounds."*
- *A sentence that compares frogs to toads is, "Frogs have moist, slimy skin, while toads have dry, bumpy skin."*
- *I know Alaska is larger than Texas because the text says: "Alaska is 663,268 square miles, which is nearly twice the size of Texas."*

COMPREHENSION HELPER

Context Clues

Hints readers use to figure out the meaning of an unknown word in a text. Context clues can come before or after the unknown word.

TIP Authors use many words you may not know. But nearby words and sentences can offer important clues to the unfamiliar word's definition. As you read, play detective and search for clues to the meaning of the mystery word. This will help you improve your understanding and vocabulary without reaching for a dictionary.

Examples

- **Definition Clues:** *The unknown word is defined in the text.*
- **Example Clues:** *An example of the unknown word is provided in the text.*
- **Synonym Clues:** *A word with a similar meaning is near the unknown word.*
- **Antonym Clues:** *A word with the opposite meaning is near the unknown word.*

COMPREHENSION HELPER

Inference

Drawing a conclusion about a text based on clues within it.

TIP Text clues are words or details that help you figure out an unstated idea. To make an inference, combine clues in the text with your own background knowledge to figure out what the author is *really* trying to tell you.

Examples

- *If a nonfiction book says, "Harriet Tubman walked through the dangerous, dark woods all by herself," you could **infer** that she was very brave.*
- *If an article states, "Sugar tastes sweet, but too much of it can have sour consequences," you could **infer** that eating lots of sugar is bad for your health.*
- *If a memoir reads, "As a kid, I was always by myself, which made me sad," you could **infer** that the writer was a lonely child.*

100 INFORMATIONAL TASK CARDS

What Can a Dog's Tail Tell You?

Most people think a dog's tail tells just one thing: A wagging tail means the dog is happy. But in fact, dogs' tails have a lot to say. Sometimes a wagging tail does mean a dog is happy, but only when the tail wags to the right! A wag to the left, on the other hand, means the dog is upset or stressed out. A dog that's very scared might tuck its tail under its body. And when a dog is feeling angry or **aggressive**, it often holds its tail straight up. Dogs may not

be able to talk, but if we pay attention to their tails, we can understand them anyway!

KEY QUESTIONS

1. MAIN IDEA: What is the main idea?

2. DETAILS: What is an important detail?

3. TEXT EVIDENCE: What does it mean when a dog wags its tail to the left? Cite the text.

4. CONTEXT CLUES: What do you think *aggressive* means?

☐ tired
☐ mean
☐ hungry

5. S-T-R-E-T-C-H: Can you think of another title that would work for this story? Tell why you picked it.

Hard Work Pays Off

Some people believe that if they don't get good at something quickly, they never will be good at it. But in just about every area, from art to zoology, hard work pays off. Of course, some people are good at things **right off the bat**. Some excel at math without even trying. Others are naturally good at music or sports. But people who aren't good at things can get better and better if they keep working at it. Today, Stephen Curry is a basketball superstar. In high school, people thought Stephen was just an average player, but he worked hard to get better. Even now, Curry says he's always trying to improve his game.

KEY QUESTIONS

1. MAIN IDEA: What is the main idea?

2. DETAILS: What is an important detail?

3. TEXT EVIDENCE: Does Stephen Curry still work hard? Cite the text.

4. CONTEXT CLUES: What do you think the phrase *right off the bat* means?

☐ frequently
☐ right away
☐ in baseball

5. S-T-R-E-T-C-H: What skill have you worked hard to improve? Tell about it.

INFO TEXT: MAIN IDEA AND DETAILS

Polar Bears Out in the Cold

Temperatures in the Arctic can get down to –40 degrees Fahrenheit. That's *really* cold! But the polar bears that live there are perfectly adapted for their environment. Their fur helps them blend in with the snow and it **repels** water, so they dry off quickly. Their fur is very thick, which helps keep them warm. Underneath the fur, they have a thick layer of fat, which also serves to keep them warm. And unlike other bears that eat whatever they can find, polar bears eat only fatty animals, like seals and walruses. This, too, helps ensure that they eat enough calories to stay nice and toasty.

KEY QUESTIONS

1. MAIN IDEA: What is the main idea?

2. DETAILS: What is an important detail?

3. CONTRAST: What is one way polar bears are different from other bears?

4. CONTEXT CLUES: What do you think *repels* means?

☐ drinks
☐ gathers
☒ keeps away

5. S-T-R-E-T-C-H: Do you think you are well suited to live in the Arctic? Why or why not?

because human can't survive ... the polar bears

INFO TEXT: MAIN IDEA AND DETAILS

The World's Biggest Marathon

Hundreds of marathons take place every year, but New York City's is by far the largest. Every November, thousands of people lace up their sneakers in the Big Apple and hit the road. And they *keep* hitting it for 26.2 miles! In 2015, nearly 50,000 runners crossed the finish line. People of all ages and athletic abilities run the NYC race—some who run fast, some who run slowly, some who walk, and even some who race in wheelchairs. The New York City Marathon draws runners from all over the world. And each year, as many as two million **spectators** come out to cheer them on.

KEY QUESTIONS

1. MAIN IDEA: What is the main idea?

2. DETAILS: What is an important detail?

3. TEXT EVIDENCE: Do you have to be a New Yorker to run in the New York City Marathon? Cite the text.

4. CONTEXT CLUES: What do you think *spectators* means?

☐ glasses
☐ runners
☒ watchers

5. S-T-R-E-T-C-H: Would you like to run in the New York City Marathon? Why or why not?

Yes, because running 26.2 miles seems good 4 you

Beetles, Beetles, Everywhere!

There are so many beetles. There are nearly 400,000 different types of these insects. That means there are more beetles than any other creature on Earth. Beetles come in all different colors: red, yellow, orange, green, and even purple. They live in a variety of **habitats**—from cold polar regions to hot deserts. Some beetles are pests that eat farmers' crops. Others are helpful because they eat other insects. The largest beetle is the Titan, which lives in the rain forest. It can grow to be eight inches long. The smallest is the featherwing beetle. You would need a microscope to see it. Yes, the whole world is crawling with beetles!

KEY QUESTIONS

1. MAIN IDEA: What is the main idea?

2. DETAILS: What is an important detail?

3. TEXT EVIDENCE: Do some beetles create problems for farmers? Cite the text.

4. CONTEXT CLUES: What do you think *habitats* means?

- [ ] houses
- [ ] homes
- [ ] valleys

5. S-T-R-E-T-C-H: What is your favorite insect? Tell why.

The World's Most Popular Monument

Every year, seven million people visit the Eiffel Tower in Paris, France. That makes it the world's most popular monument. It gets more visitors than Mount Rushmore or the Great Pyramids. The Eiffel Tower was built in 1889. It's named after Gustave Eiffel, the man who designed it. For many years, it was the tallest artificial structure on Earth. Then, people began building skyscrapers that are taller. Still,  the Eiffel Tower remains a **lofty** 1,063 feet tall. To get to the top, there are 1,665 steps to climb. Fortunately, all those visitors can also take an elevator.

KEY QUESTIONS

1. MAIN IDEA: What is the main idea?

2. DETAILS: What is an important detail?

3. INFERENCE: Why did the author say, "Fortunately, all those visitors can also take an elevator"?

4. CONTEXT CLUES: What do you think *lofty* means?

- [ ] high
- [ ] strong
- [ ] beautiful

5. S-T-R-E-T-C-H: What is your favorite monument? Tell about it.

INFO TEXT: MAIN IDEA AND DETAILS

Your Fingerprints Are Yours Alone

In most ways, your fingers are pretty much like everybody else's. But in one very important way, they're not. People's fingerprints are completely **unique**, unlike anybody else's in the whole world. Even identical twins have different fingerprints! There *are* some common fingerprint patterns. Some people have loops, some have arches, and some have whorls, or circles. But the exact pattern is different for every single person, as unique as a face. Fingerprints even help police identify criminals. After a crime, police use a powder to reveal the fingerprints left behind. Because each set of prints can only belong to one person, experts can identify the criminal.

KEY QUESTIONS

1. MAIN IDEA: What is the main idea?

2. DETAILS: What is an important detail?

3. TEXT EVIDENCE: Do identical twins have the same fingerprints? Cite the text.

4. CONTEXT CLUES: What do you think *unique* means?

☐ special
☐ tiny
☐ looped

5. S-T-R-E-T-C-H: In the future, your fingerprint may become your signature. Do you like that idea? Why or why not?

INFO TEXT: MAIN IDEA AND DETAILS

A Very Special Star

Here's an important fact to know: The Sun is a star! The reason the Sun appears so large is that it is closer to the Earth than the billions of other stars. The Sun is about 93 million miles away, which makes it the Earth's close neighbor in the incredible **vastness** of space. Like other stars, the Sun is very hot—way hotter than an oven. But it takes about eight minutes for the Sun's light to travel to the Earth. By that time, the Sun's light has cooled down. And that makes it the perfect temperature for life on Earth. So next time you look up at the Sun, remember it is also a very special star.

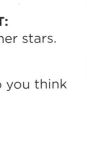

KEY QUESTIONS

1. MAIN IDEA: What is the main idea?

2. DETAILS: What is an important detail?

3. COMPARE AND CONTRAST: Name a way the Sun is like other stars. Name a way it is different.

4. CONTEXT CLUES: What do you think *vastness* means?

☐ hotness
☐ sadness
☐ largeness

5. S-T-R-E-T-C-H: Why do you think the author gave this passage the title "A Very Special Star"?

A Fad Called the Hula Hoop

There have been many **fads**, such as yo-yos and the Minecraft video game. But the hula hoop is one of the biggest ever. In 1958, this simple plastic ring went on sale in stores. It was based on hoops used by kids long ago in places like Egypt and Greece. It became a huge hit! 100 million hula hoops were quickly sold. It seemed like everyone owned one. All over America, contests were held to see how long people could keep a hula hoop spinning around their hips. Then, as quickly as it became a hit, the hula hoop faded away to make room for a brand-new fad.

KEY QUESTIONS

1. MAIN IDEA: What is the main idea?

2. DETAILS: What is an important detail?

3. TEXT EVIDENCE: Were a lot of hula hoops sold? Cite the text.

4. CONTEXT CLUES: What do you think *fads* means?

☐ nests
☐ fun toys
☐ trends

5. S-T-R-E-T-C-H: What fad have you noticed? Tell about it.

Very Cool Chameleons

Chameleons are one of the world's most interesting creatures. Chameleons are lizards, closely related to other reptiles, such as alligators, snakes, and turtles. Three cool things about chameleons are their eyes, tongues, and skin. A chameleon can **rotate** each of its eyes separately. That means it can look around in two different directions at the same time. When it spots an insect, a chameleon shoots out its long tongue. *Zap*—lunchtime! Its tongue is twice as long as its body, with a tip that sticks to prey. Best of all: Chameleons can change their skin color. Some can turn yellow, orange, blue, or even purple. Wow! Now you know why chameleons are so amazing.

KEY QUESTIONS

1. MAIN IDEA: What is the main idea?

2. DETAILS: What is an important detail?

3. INFERENCE: Why did the author write "*Zap*—lunchtime!"? What does that mean?

4. CONTEXT CLUES: What do you think *rotate* means?

☐ blink a lot
☐ move in a circle
☐ fall down

5. S-T-R-E-T-C-H: Describe a creature you think is amazing.

INFO TEXT: SEQUENCE OF EVENTS

Making Bread

Making a loaf of bread is easier than you might think. All you need is flour, water, yeast, and a pinch of sugar. The first step is to dissolve the yeast in water with a little sugar. The yeast needs the sugar to help make the dough rise. Next, you add flour and stir to make a dough. Then you put the dough on a floured surface and **knead** it with your hands for several minutes until it's no longer sticky. After that, the dough has to rest for about an hour. During that time, the dough rises and expands. Lastly, you put the bread in a pan and pop it in the oven to bake. *Mmmmm!*

KEY QUESTIONS

1. SEQUENCE: What is the first step to making bread?

2. SEQUENCE: What is the last step in making bread?

3. TEXT EVIDENCE: What happens while the dough is resting? Cite the text.

4. CONTEXT CLUES: What do you think *knead* means?

☐ bake
☐ cool
☐ pound

5. S-T-R-E-T-C-H: Have you ever baked something? Tell about it.

INFO TEXT: SEQUENCE OF EVENTS

Rihanna's Dress

The singer Rihanna once wore a dress that took two years to make! It was created by Guo Pei, one of the most famous designers in China. To get started, Pei took Rihanna's measurements. Next, Pei picked out a fabric for the dress. Then, she spent two whole years **meticulously** sewing it by hand. Rihanna's dress was gold-colored with fur and a long train that dragged across the floor. The dress weighed 55 pounds! Rihanna wore it to a ball in New York City in 2015. It was a big hit for Rihanna and for Pei, too.

KEY QUESTIONS

1. SEQUENCE: What was the first step in making Rihanna's dress?

2. SEQUENCE: After taking Rihanna's measurements, what did the designer do?

3. DETAILS: What country is Guo Pei from?

4. VOCABULARY: What do you think *meticulously* means?

☐ very carefully
☐ very loudly
☐ very stylishly

5. S-T-R-E-T-C-H: What would you enjoy meticulously working on for two years? Tell about it.

What a Life!

The life of a 17-year cicada is an amazing journey. When an adult female is ready, she lays hundreds of eggs in a branch of a tree. About eight weeks later, the eggs hatch. The newly hatched nymphs fall to the ground. Then they **burrow** about a foot underground. That spot is where they stay for the next 17 years, feeding on the sap of the tree's roots. When 17 years have passed, the cicadas emerge from the ground by the thousands. As they climb the very tree where they hatched 17 years earlier, they shed their outer skins. Then they're ready to begin the cycle all over again!

KEY QUESTIONS

1. SEQUENCE: What happens first in the 17-year cicada's life cycle?

2. SEQUENCE: What do the nymphs do after they fall to the ground?

3. INFERENCE: Why are these insects called "17-year cicadas"?

4. CONTEXT CLUES: What do you think *burrow* means?

☐ dig down
☐ loan
☐ wait

5. S-T-R-E-T-C-H: Would you like to be present when the cicadas emerge from the ground? Why or why not?

Write On!

Would you like to write fiction? First, brainstorm until you come up with a really great story idea. Then write a first draft. This draft might be kind of messy, but it's good to get the basic story down in writing. Next, edit your draft. The editing stage is the chance to make important changes. Maybe you want to change a character, or perhaps you've thought of a great new twist for the ending. Keep editing your piece of fiction until it's polished. Last, but not least, proofread your work to make sure the grammar and spelling are perfect. **Voilà!** Now, you have a story. Don't forget to share your story with friends and classmates.

KEY QUESTIONS

1. SEQUENCE: What is the first step in writing fiction?

2. SEQUENCE: What is the last step in writing fiction?

3. MAIN IDEA: What is the main idea of this passage?

4. CONTEXT CLUES: What do you think *Voilà!* means?

☐ Write on!
☐ So sorry!
☐ There it is!

5. S-T-R-E-T-C-H: What is your favorite step in the writing process? Why?

INFO TEXT: SEQUENCE OF EVENTS

How Bees Make Honey

You probably know that bees make honey, but how exactly do they do it? It all starts with flowers. When a honeybee lands on a flower, it drinks in the flower's nectar—a sweet juice at the flower's center. The bee stores the nectar in its stomach. Then it moves on to more and more flowers. Once its stomach is completely full, it flies back to the hive. There, it **regurgitates** the nectar from its stomach. Other bees quickly flap their wings, which helps draw out excess moisture from the nectar, creating honey. Finally, the honey is put into a honeycomb made of beeswax.

KEY QUESTIONS

1. SEQUENCE: What's the first thing a bee does in order to make honey?

2. SEQUENCE: What is the final step in the honey-making process?

3. AUTHOR'S PURPOSE: Is the author's purpose to inform or persuade you?

4. CONTEXT CLUES: What do you think *regurgitates* means?

- ☐ swallows
- ☐ spits up
- ☐ flies

5. S-T-R-E-T-C-H: How do honeybees help people? How can they hurt people? Tell about it.

INFO TEXT: SEQUENCE OF EVENTS

Getting Behind the Wheel

When teens turn 16, they're old enough to drive. But before they become legal drivers they have to follow certain steps. First, they have to take a driver's education class. That's where they learn the rules of the road. Next, they get their learner's permit. This permit **authorizes** them to drive as long as there's an adult in the car. The next step is putting in months of driving practice. Finally, when they feel ready, they take an official driving test. If they pass, they get their driver's license. If they fail, they can continue to practice and retake the test.

KEY QUESTIONS

1. SEQUENCE: What's the first thing teens must do to get their driver's license?

2. SEQUENCE: What do they do after they get their learner's permit?

3. TEXT EVIDENCE: What can teens do if they fail the driving test? Cite the text.

4. CONTEXT CLUES: What do you think *authorizes* means?

- ☐ allows
- ☐ signs
- ☐ prevents

5. S-T-R-E-T-C-H: Do you think it should be easier to get a driver's license? Why or why not?

INFO TEXT: SEQUENCE OF EVENTS

Smoothie Time!

Here's how to make a delicious fruit smoothie. First, put some ice in a blender. Then add some plain yogurt. You can also add a little honey if you'd like a sweeter smoothie. Next, put a banana in the blender. After that comes the real fun. You get to decide what other fruits go in your smoothie: strawberries, blueberries, pineapple, mango, or kiwi. There are so many choices of fruit! You can even mix a bunch of different fruits if you like. Now, run  the blender until everything is well mixed and **frothy**. Great! You're almost finished. But there's one last, important step: Drink your delicious smoothie.

KEY QUESTIONS

1. SEQUENCE: What is the first step in making a smoothie?

2. SEQUENCE: What is the very last step?

3. TEXT EVIDENCE: Are there few choices of fruits for smoothies? Cite the text.

4. CONTEXT CLUES: What do you think *frothy* means?

☐ sweet and sour
☐ light and foamy
☐ dark and salty

5. S-T-R-E-T-C-H: What is your idea of a perfect smoothie? Make a list of all ingredients.

INFO TEXT: SEQUENCE OF EVENTS

Biking Through the Years

In 1817, a contraption called a bicycle was invented in Germany. Soon, bikes were on a roll. Inventors started coming up with different versions. In 1870, the first high-wheelers appeared. You've probably seen pictures of these funny-looking bikes with a huge front wheel and tiny wheel in back. In 1878, the first bikes were made in America. Over the years, bikes have continued to **evolve**. In 1978, for example, the  first mountain bike was created. What kind of bike do you think will be created next?

KEY QUESTIONS

1. SEQUENCE: When and where was the bicycle invented?

2. SEQUENCE: What is the last type of bike mentioned in the text?

3. DETAILS: What year did high-wheelers first appear?

4. CONTEXT CLUES: What do you think *evolve* means?

☐ change and improve
☐ spin and spin
☐ rock and roll

5. S-T-R-E-T-C-H: Use your imagination to "invent" a brand-new bike. What does it look like? What can it do?

Learn to Whistle!

Do you know how to whistle? If not, here are some steps to follow. With practice, you'll soon be able to whistle like a teakettle! Stand in front of a mirror so you can **observe** the shape of your mouth. Wet your lips and say, "ooh." Notice the shape of your mouth. Your lips should form a small circle. Curl your tongue up and away from your teeth. Now, try blowing a stream of air through the opening of your lips. Do you hear anything? If not, don't worry. It can take a while to get the hang of it. The last step is to keep practicing.

KEY QUESTIONS

1. SEQUENCE: What is the first step in learning how to whistle?

2. SEQUENCE: What is the second step?

3. FIGURATIVE LANGUAGE: A simile compares two unlike things using the word *like* or *as*. *Hop like a frog* is a simile. Can you find one in the story?

4. CONTEXT CLUES: What do you think *observe* means?

- ☐ blow
- ☐ shape
- ☐ watch

5. S-T-R-E-T-C-H: What is something else you've taught yourself to do? Tell about it.

Butterfly Life Cycle

Flutter, flutter! The first step in the butterfly life cycle occurs when a butterfly lays an egg on a leaf. Next, the egg hatches, and a baby caterpillar **emerges**. The caterpillar feeds on leaves and quickly grows. After it has gotten much larger, the caterpillar hangs upside down from a leaf. A hard shell, called a chrysalis, forms around the caterpillar. Inside the chrysalis, the creature starts to change. It grows wings. It also develops a long, straw-like tongue, called a proboscis, to drink from flowers. After about 10 days, the chrysalis cracks open. Out comes a beautiful butterfly. Flutter, flutter!

KEY QUESTIONS

1. SEQUENCE: What is the first step in the butterfly life cycle?

2. SEQUENCE: What happens right after that?

3. DETAILS: What is a butterfly's long, straw-like tongue called?

4. CONTEXT CLUES: What do you think *emerges* means?

- ☐ flies away
- ☐ eats a lot
- ☐ comes out

5. S-T-R-E-T-C-H: Do you think a butterfly is the best insect? If not, what is? Explain your choice.

INFO TEXT: SUMMARIZE

The Bay Bridge Series

The nickname for the 1989 World Series was "the Bay Bridge Series." The two teams in the series were the Oakland A's and the San Francisco Giants. Oakland and San Francisco are separated by water, and the cities are connected by the Bay Bridge. The A's were leading the series, but on the night of Game 3, things got shaken up—literally! Just before the game was about to start, an earthquake struck. It measured 6.9 on the Richter scale—which means it was a very strong **jolt**. No one at the game was hurt, but elsewhere the earthquake caused serious damage. The game was postponed and was played 10 days later.

KEY QUESTIONS

1. SUMMARIZE: Summarize this passage in a few sentences.

2. INFERENCE: Why was the series called the Bay Bridge Series?

3. TEXT EVIDENCE: Did the earthquake cause any damage? Cite the text.

4. CONTEXT CLUES: What do you think *jolt* means?

☐ disaster
☐ experience
☐ shake

5. S-T-R-E-T-C-H: What is your favorite sport to watch? Why?

INFO TEXT: SUMMARIZE

Meet the Liger

What do you get if you cross a lion and a tiger? A liger! And yes, that's a real animal. Ligers have stripes like tigers. They have manes like lions. However, ligers don't exist in the wild. That's because lions and tigers don't live in the same habitats. Ligers are only born in places like zoos. They're the **offspring** of a male lion and a female tiger. They also happen to be the world's largest cats. Ligers can be more than 10 feet long and weigh 1,000 pounds. Now, that's one big kitty!

KEY QUESTIONS

1. SUMMARIZE: Summarize this passage in a few sentences.

2. COMPARE AND CONTRAST: How are ligers like tigers? How are they different?

3. TEXT EVIDENCE: How big is a liger? Cite the text.

4. CONTEXT CLUES: What do you think *offspring* means?

☐ children
☐ pets
☐ uncles

5. S-T-R-E-T-C-H: If you could cross two animals, which would you choose and why?

A Hero Named Frederick Douglass

Frederick Douglass was a great and courageous man. He was born into slavery in Maryland in 1818. He was soon separated from his mother, and he never knew his father. During the time of slavery, it was illegal for enslaved people to learn how to read. But when Frederick was 12, the wife of his owner taught him the alphabet. Later, Frederick secretly continued his lessons on his own. He taught others to read, too. Then, when he was 20, he escaped to the North where there was no slavery. He became an **abolitionist**, writing books about his life and working to permanently end slavery in this country.

KEY QUESTIONS

1. SUMMARIZE: Summarize this passage in a few sentences.

2. INFERENCE: Why did Douglass continue his lessons in secret?

3. DETAILS: What year was Douglass born?

4. CONTEXT CLUES: What do you think *abolitionist* means?

☐ someone who reads books
☐ someone who takes risks
☐ someone who works to end slavery

5. S-T-R-E-T-C-H: Why do you think it was illegal for enslaved people to learn to read?

For Brave Climbers Only!

Mt. Everest is the highest mountain on Earth. It's part of the Himalayan mountain range in Asia. Everest stands 29,029 feet tall. That means its peak is more than five miles up in the air! But that hasn't stopped people from risking death to climb it. They have to use ropes, ice axes, and special boots. The climb is very dangerous, so they have to go very slowly and carefully. When climbers arrive at the **summit**, they get an unforgettable view from the top of the world. After that, it's time to begin the long, careful journey back down.

KEY QUESTIONS

1. SUMMARIZE: Summarize this passage in a few sentences.

2. TEXT EVIDENCE: Where is Mt. Everest located? Cite the text.

3. INFERENCE: Why is the title "For Brave Climbers Only!"?

4. CONTEXT CLUES: What do you think *summit* means?

☐ the bottom
☐ the middle
☐ the top

5. S-T-R-E-T-C-H: Would you like to climb Mt. Everest? Why or why not?

Theodore *Who?*

You may not recognize the name Theodore Geisel, but you've probably read a few of his books: *The Cat in the Hat*, *Green Eggs and Ham*, *Hop on Pop*. Dr. Seuss is the author's name on these famous books, but that was a **pseudonym**. His actual name was Theodore Geisel. Before he began writing children's books, Geisel worked as an illustrator and cartoonist. He was in his 40s when he wrote and illustrated his first book. It was called *And to Think That I Saw It on Mulberry Street*. That's when he began using the pen name Dr. Seuss.

Geisel went on to write and illustrate 43 more books. He also became one of the best-loved children's book writers ever.

KEY QUESTIONS

1. SUMMARIZE: Summarize this passage in a few sentences.

2. TEXT EVIDENCE: How old was Theodore Geisel when he wrote his first book? Cite the text.

3. INFERENCE: How many books did Geisel write in all?

4. CONTEXT CLUES: What do you think *pseudonym* means?

☐ cartoon
☐ author
☐ secret name

5. S-T-R-E-T-C-H: If you had a pseudonym, what would it be? Why?

Extra, Extra!

In the old days, children often had to work to make money for their families. A common job for boys was selling newspapers. These boys, some as young as five, were called "newsies." In 1899, the New York City newsies went on strike and refused to sell papers. They were angry because their pay was so low. Some days they worked until midnight and only made 30 cents! The newsies gave speeches, chanted **slogans** saying they would "stick together like glue," and marched across the Brooklyn Bridge. After two weeks, the newspapers agreed to raise their pay. The newsies were young, but they were powerful!

KEY QUESTIONS

1. SUMMARIZE: Summarize this passage in a few sentences.

2. INFERENCE: In the last sentence, why are the newsies described as "powerful"?

3. PROBLEM AND SOLUTION: What was the newsies' problem? How did they solve it?

4. CONTEXT CLUES: What do you think *slogans* means?

☐ boring words
☐ silly stories
☐ memorable words

5. S-T-R-E-T-C-H: If you had to work, what job would you choose and why?

INFO TEXT: SUMMARIZE

Is There Anybody Out There?

Have you ever wondered if there is life on other planets? Scientists are pretty sure that there isn't life on the other planets in our own solar system. But what about planets farther away? In recent years, **astronomers** have discovered that there are many, many more planets out in space than they once believed. In fact, there are trillions and trillions! These planets are too far away for scientists to study. But, they do know that some of them orbit around a sun in a position much like Earth's. That means that some of these faraway planets could be home to life-forms. Maybe one day, we'll find out for sure.

KEY QUESTIONS

1. SUMMARIZE: Summarize this passage in a few sentences.

2. MAIN IDEA: What is the main idea?

3. INFERENCE: Why is the passage titled "Is There Anybody Out There?"

4. CONTEXT CLUES: What do you think *astronomers* means?

☐ scientists who study space
☐ astronauts
☐ school teachers

5. S-T-R-E-T-C-H: Do you think there's life on other planets? Why or why not?

INFO TEXT: SUMMARIZE

The Importance of Sleep

Sleeping can seem like a big waste of time. You lie down and, for 10 hours, you do absolutely nothing! Just think of all the fun stuff you could be doing! But the truth is, sleep is very important. It may seem like you're not doing anything when you **hit the hay**, but in fact you're recharging your brain and repairing your body's cells. Most experts think that kids need 10 to 11 hours of sleep each night. Kids who get more sleep are healthier, happier, and do

 better in school. Those sound like good reasons to get your *zzzz*'s.

KEY QUESTIONS

1. SUMMARIZE: Summarize this passage in a few sentences.

2. MAIN IDEA: What is the main idea?

3. CAUSE AND EFFECT: What are three effects of getting more sleep?

4. CONTEXT CLUES: What do you think the phrase *hit the hay* means?

☐ exercise
☐ go to bed
☐ eat dinner

5. S-T-R-E-T-C-H: Describe how you feel when you don't get enough sleep.

The Crossroads of the World

Times Square is a busy spot in the middle of New York City. It is nicknamed the "crossroads of the world" because tourists from all over the world walk through it. Giant billboards light the sky. There are musicians playing guitars and dancers doing hip-hop. There are cheers and tips placed in passed hats. There are street **vendors** selling pretzels. Each year on New Year's Eve, about a million people gather in Times Square for a ceremony. They count down as a big crystal ball is slowly lowered. Maybe you've seen this on television: 5, 4, 3, 2, 1 . . . Happy New Year!

KEY QUESTIONS

1. SUMMARIZE: Summarize this passage in a few sentences.

2. TEXT EVIDENCE: Are there advertising signs in Times Square? Cite the text.

3. INFERENCE: Why are tips being placed in passed hats?

4. CONTEXT CLUES: What do you think *vendors* means?

☐ people eating food
☐ people selling things
☐ people laughing loudly

5. S-T-R-E-T-C-H: Would you like to visit Times Square? Why or why not?

The Great Jackie Robinson

In 1947, Jackie Robinson joined the Brooklyn Dodgers. He was the first African American to play major league baseball. That wasn't easy. People in the crowd would often yell cruel things. Some of the players were disrespectful, too. But not only was Robinson a talented ballplayer, he was also very brave. He didn't let the foolish behavior of others bother him. He simply played baseball. Over time, his **admirable** character won the respect of everyone. Robinson became a big star. He played for many years. In 1962, he became a member of the Baseball Hall of Fame. Robinson was a great baseball player and an even greater American.

KEY QUESTIONS

1. SUMMARIZE: Summarize this passage in a few sentences.

2. TEXT EVIDENCE: Did Robinson play baseball for only a short time? Cite the text.

3. DETAILS: What year did Robinson join the Baseball Hall of Fame?

4. CONTEXT CLUES: What do you think *admirable* means?

☐ someone in the Navy
☐ enviable
☐ deserving of great respect

5. S-T-R-E-T-C-H: Why might someone consider Robinson even greater as an American than as a baseball player?

Basketball and Soccer

In 1891, James Naismith invented the game of basketball. He was partly inspired by soccer. Both   sports are played in a rectangular area. In both sports, the ball can go out of bounds. Soccer and basketball each have nets. But there are some big differences, too. Basketball uses the **term** "point" for scoring, while in soccer it's called a "goal." Basketball players use their hands, while soccer players use their feet. In basketball, the scoring is constant. It's not unusual for a team to reach 100 points. Scoring even one goal in soccer can be super challenging. A soccer match might end up in a 0-0 tie. Which sport do you like better?

KEY QUESTIONS

1. COMPARE: How are basketball and soccer similar?

2. CONTRAST: How are they different?

3. TEXT EVIDENCE: Did Michael Jordan invent the game of basketball? Cite the text.

4. CONTEXT CLUES: What do you think *term* means?

☐ a kind of bird
☐ a word that describes
☐ a fun puzzle

5. S-T-R-E-T-C-H: Compare and contrast soccer with a different sport, such as football.

What's the Difference Between Tortoises and Turtles?

Did you know that turtles and tortoises are different species? Although they have lots of similarities, there are some differences between them. Both creatures are reptiles, and both are covered with hard shells. Turtles' shells tend to be less rounded than tortoises' shells. Tortoises' shells are much more **dome-shaped**. Another difference between these creatures is their habitat. Turtles spend some or most of their time in water, while tortoises live on land. They also have different diets. Tortoises eat only plants, but turtles eat plants and animals. Now you know how to tell these amazing creatures apart!

KEY QUESTIONS

1. COMPARE: How are turtles and tortoises similar?

2. CONTRAST: How are they different?

3. MAIN IDEA: What is the main idea of this passage?

4. CONTEXT CLUES: What do you think *dome-shaped* means?

☐ rounded
☐ long
☐ soft

5. S-T-R-E-T-C-H: Do you think you would ever see a tortoise swimming? Why?

The Way to Go

If you wanted to visit someone far away, how would you get there? You might fly in an airplane. Or you might take a train. Both **modes** of travel are safe and will get you where you're going. Planes, however, travel much faster than trains, so you get to your destination sooner. Trains travel slowly and make lots of stops along the way. If plane travel is so much faster, why do some people still choose trains? One reason is price. Train travel is often cheaper. Also, train passengers get to see the scenery—something people can't do when they're 37,000 feet up in the air.

KEY QUESTIONS

1. COMPARE: How are plane travel and train travel similar?

2. CONTRAST: How are they different?

3. DETAILS: Name two reasons someone might choose a train over a plane.

4. CONTEXT CLUES: What do you think *modes* means?

☐ ways
☐ places
☐ differences

5. S-T-R-E-T-C-H: Compare and contrast two other forms of transportation.

Two Ways to Make Music

An orchestra is a big group that plays music together. Orchestras tend to play classical music. Some orchestras feature more than 100 musicians arranged in sections. There's usually a strings section featuring violin players and harpists. There's usually a brass section with horns and tubas. The conductor makes sure all the sections work together. Bands are usually smaller than orchestras. Some have only three or four members. They play other musical styles, such as rock, jazz, salsa, and reggae. If you attend an orchestra performance, expect to sit quietly and to listen **intently**. If you see a band, you might just jump up and start dancing.

KEY QUESTIONS

1. COMPARE: How are orchestras and bands similar?

2. CONTRAST: How are they different?

3. DETAILS: Name four instruments you will likely find in an orchestra.

4. CONTEXT CLUES: What do you think *intently* means?

☐ loudly
☐ musically
☐ carefully

5. S-T-R-E-T-C-H: If you had a band, what would you name it and what kind of music would you play?

See Ya Later, Alligator!

Alligators and crocodiles look a lot alike. They belong to the group of reptiles called Crocodilia. Both are related to dinosaurs. Crocodiles and alligators have lived on Earth for millions of years! So how are they different? A crocodile's **snout** is usually longer and V-shaped, while an alligator's snout is usually shorter and U-shaped. Alligators are dark gray, while crocodiles are brownish green. Gators like fresh water, but crocs prefer salt water. Crocodiles are bigger and live longer than alligators. And lastly, even when a croc's mouth is shut, two of its lower teeth are visible. You can't see a gator's teeth unless its jaws are wide open.

KEY QUESTIONS

1. COMPARE: How are alligators and crocodiles similar?

2. CONTRAST: How are they different?

3. TEXT EVIDENCE: What reptile group do crocodiles and alligators belong to? Cite the text.

4. CONTEXT CLUES: What do you think *snout* means?

☐ eyes and ears
☐ nose and mouth
☐ front legs

5. S-T-R-E-T-C-H: Snakes and lizards are reptiles, too. Compare and contrast them.

Great Entertainment

Would you rather read a book or watch a movie? Both are fun to do, and each has its

advantages. Both can tell great stories. They can be funny, exciting, scary, or suspenseful. They can **transport** you to other times and other worlds. But books and movies are obviously very different. Movies are filmed. You watch the action as it unfolds on the screen. All you have to do is sit back and enjoy. Books, on the other hand, take a little more work. When you read, you picture the scenes in your head. You use your imagination to picture everything the author is telling you. Which do you prefer?

KEY QUESTIONS

1. COMPARE: How are books and movies similar?

2. CONTRAST: How are they different?

3. MAIN IDEA: What's the main idea of this passage?

4. CONTEXT CLUES: What do you think *transport* means?

☐ describe
☐ carry
☐ frighten

5. S-T-R-E-T-C-H: Do you prefer movies or books? Tell why.

Pass the Veggies, Please!

Humans are natural omnivores, which means they can eat both animals and plants. But some people choose to be vegetarian. They eat fruits and vegetables, dairy, grains, and eggs, but they never eat meat or fish. They may eat this way because they think it's healthier, or because they don't want to harm animals. Other people are vegan. Vegans follow an even more **restricted** diet. Like vegetarians, they avoid eating meat, but they also avoid any foods that come from animals.

That includes eggs and dairy. Many vegans also avoid wearing leather. Most vegans are motivated by a concern for animals and the environment.

KEY QUESTIONS

1. COMPARE: How are vegetarians and vegans similar?

2. CONTRAST: How are they different?

3. TEXT EVIDENCE: Why are some people vegan? Cite the text.

4. CONTEXT CLUES: What do you think *restricted* means?
- [ ] funny
- [ ] delicious
- [ ] limited

5. S-T-R-E-T-C-H: Would you ever become a vegetarian or vegan? Why or why not?

Boats, Small and Big

Rowboats and cruise ships are types of boats. Both are fun ways for people to travel in the water. However, rowboats are small. They are **propelled** using oars and can hold just a few people at most. But a rowboat sure is perfect if you want to go fishing in a lake. Cruise ships are gigantic. Propelled by powerful engines, they can carry thousands of passengers. Entertainment, like movies and magic shows, can be seen right on the ship, and there are even rooms to sleep in at night. A cruise ship is perfect if you want to cross an entire ocean—and have fun doing it!

KEY QUESTIONS

1. COMPARE: How are rowboats and cruise ships similar?

2. CONTRAST: How are they different?

3. TEXT EVIDENCE: Are cruise ships a good choice for long trips? Cite the text.

4. CONTEXT CLUES: What do you think *propelled* means?
- [ ] soaked
- [ ] moved
- [ ] stopped

5. S-T-R-E-T-C-H: Would you prefer to spend the day in a rowboat or a cruise ship? Why?

Two Great States

Rhode Island is famous for its beaches. Alaska is known for its wilderness. Rhode Island is the smallest state. Alaska is the largest. Alaska is so large that you could actually fit 425 Rhode Islands inside of it! In fact, Alaska is so very huge that it makes up one-fifth of the total size of America. But tiny Rhode Island and giant Alaska also share some things in common. Both states have a small **population**. About a million people live in Rhode Island. About 750,000 people live in Alaska. Both states also get plenty of snow. That said, huge, cold Alaska gets a whole lot more of it!

KEY QUESTIONS

1. COMPARE: How are Rhode Island and Alaska similar?

2. CONTRAST: How are they different?

3. TEXT EVIDENCE: Do 100 people live in Rhode Island?

4. CONTEXT CLUES: What do you think *population* means?

☐ air pollution
☐ amount of people living in an area
☐ forest and trees

5. S-T-R-E-T-C-H: Compare and contrast two other states.

Email Versus Regular Mail

Two ways you can send items are email and regular mail. Email is a lot faster. When you send a message, it arrives almost **instantaneously**. Regular mail, also known as snail mail, often takes a couple of days. You can send lots of things by email, not just messages. You can also email an online birthday card, a video, or a song. But regular mail is the only choice for sending an actual object, like a box of candy or even a bicycle! When it's your birthday and packages come to your home, aren't you glad for snail mail?

KEY QUESTIONS

1. COMPARE: How are email and regular mail similar?

2. CONTRAST: How are they different?

3. INFERENCE: Why is regular mail sometimes called "snail mail"?

4. CONTEXT CLUES: What do you think *instantaneously* means?

☐ immediately
☐ overnight
☐ in the same language

5. S-T-R-E-T-C-H: What is the best thing you ever got via email or regular mail? Tell about it.

Jumping Heroes!

If there's a fire in a city, fire engines roar to the scene. What happens if there's a fire out in the wilderness, where there are no roads for fire trucks? How can firefighters get there? The answer is by airplane. Smokejumpers are special firefighters who leap out of airplanes and parachute down to earth. Because forest fires are gigantic, it takes many days to put them out. Teams of smokejumpers fight fires all day and camp at night. They keep fighting until the fire is **extinguished**. The first time smokejumpers were used was in 1939. They are still some of the bravest people around.

KEY QUESTIONS

1. PROBLEM: What problem is described in this passage?

2. SOLUTION: How is it solved?

3. TEXT EVIDENCE: What year did smokejumpers start fighting fires? Cite the text.

4. CONTEXT CLUES: What do you think *extinguished* means?

☐ made larger
☐ burned up
☐ put out

5. S-T-R-E-T-C-H: Would you like to be a smokejumper? Tell why or why not.

Malaria Nets Make a Big Difference

In some countries around the world, a disease called malaria can make people very sick. The disease doesn't occur in the United States, but it is common in countries around the globe. The disease is carried by mosquitoes. When they bite people, they can **transmit** the malaria virus, and people get sick. Mosquitoes often bite at night when people are sleeping. So one way this problem has been successfully addressed is through the use of nets. The thin,  lightweight nets look like tents, and people sleep inside them. These nets keep mosquitoes away, so they can't bite people and make them sick.

KEY QUESTIONS

1. PROBLEM: What problem is described in this passage?

2. SOLUTION: How is it solved?

3. TEXT EVIDENCE: What insect carries malaria? Cite the text.

4. CONTEXT CLUES: What do you think *transmit* means?

☐ pass along
☐ scratch
☐ hold

5. S-T-R-E-T-C-H: Can you think of another invention that helps keep people healthy? Tell about it.

Scuba Diving

People cannot breathe underwater. If you hold your breath, maybe you could stay under for one minute. What if you wanted to spend more time underwater? Well, you could use scuba equipment. Scuba stands for "self-contained underwater breathing **apparatus**." There's special gear, such as goggles, flippers, and most important, a tank filled with oxygen. You'd have to take lessons to learn how to use this gear, safely. Then you could do some serious exploring. With a scuba tank, there's enough air to stay underwater for about one hour without coming up once. That gives you plenty of time to see lots of fish in a coral reef!

KEY QUESTIONS

1. PROBLEM: What problem is described in this passage?

2. SOLUTION: How is it solved?

3. TEXT EVIDENCE: Do the letters in "scuba" mean something? Cite the text.

4. CONTEXT CLUES: What do you think *apparatus* means?

☐ equipment
☐ lungs
☐ type of green vegetable

5. S-T-R-E-T-C-H: How do goggles and flippers help people underwater?

Saving the American Crocodile

Long ago, there were thousands of crocodiles living along the southern tip of Florida. But over the centuries, these animals were hunted for sport and for their skins. Some were also captured and put into zoos. By the 1970s, there were only about 200 of these mighty creatures left. It looked as though American crocodiles might become extinct. But in 1975, they were placed on the **endangered** species list, which meant it became illegal to hunt or capture them. This plan proved highly successful. In 2005, there were approximately 1,000 crocodiles living in Florida, and two years later the species was no longer considered endangered.

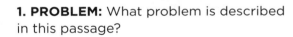

KEY QUESTIONS

1. PROBLEM: What problem is described in this passage?

2. SOLUTION: How was it solved?

3. DETAILS: How many American crocodiles were there in the 1970s?

4. CONTEXT CLUES: What do you think *endangered* means?

☐ illegal
☐ at risk of becoming extinct
☐ good for hunting

5. S-T-R-E-T-C-H: Why is it a bad thing when an animal becomes extinct?

A Park in the Air

An old railroad track ran above the streets of New York City. For many years, trains had not used this **elevated** stretch of track. It had become a dirty, rusty eyesore. Many people thought it should be torn down. But one group of New Yorkers had a very different idea—turn the old railway into a park! They cleaned and painted it, planted flowers and grasses, and added sculptures and benches. In 2009, the High Line park opened. Today, nearly five million people visit each year. The High Line is a special park in the air above the streets of New York City. What a view!

KEY QUESTIONS

1. PROBLEM: What problem is described in this passage?

2. SOLUTION: How was it solved?

3. TEXT EVIDENCE: Did the High Line open in 2016? Cite the text.

4. CONTEXT CLUES: What do you think *elevated* means?

☐ dirty
☐ stuck
☐ placed high

5. S-T-R-E-T-C-H: Why do you think this park is called the "High Line"?

Help! I've Got an Earworm!

Have you ever had an earworm? That's when you get a song stuck in your head. Maybe it's the latest hit by Meghan Trainor or Bruno Mars. The song keeps playing in your head over and over and over. Even if you like the song, this can get pretty annoying! Common advice to chase away earworms is to read a book or do a challenging puzzle, like Sudoku. But researchers in England have found that there's an even easier way to get rid of an **exasperating** earworm: chew some gum! The researchers found that chewing gum successfully kept songs from staying stuck in people's heads.

KEY QUESTIONS

1. PROBLEM: What problem is described in this passage?

2. SOLUTION: How is it solved?

3. DETAILS: What two pop stars are mentioned?

4. CONTEXT CLUES: What do you think *exasperating* means?

☐ annoying
☐ favorite
☐ English

5. S-T-R-E-T-C-H: Have you ever had an earworm? What did you do?

Lifeguards to the Rescue

Swimming first became a popular activity in the United States in the 1800s. When the first beach resorts were opened, crowds of people went to the beaches to escape the summer heat. But as the number of people going swimming went up, so did the number of people drowning! At first, police officers were called to watch out for swimmers in danger. But later, people were specially trained for water rescue, and the **vocation** of "lifeguard" was born. Today, at beaches and swimming pools around the country, lifeguards rescue more than 100,000 people from drowning every year.

KEY QUESTIONS

1. PROBLEM: What problem is described in this passage?

2. SOLUTION: How is it solved?

3. DETAILS: How many people are saved from drowning each year?

4. CONTEXT CLUES: What do you think *vocation* means?

☐ job
☐ drowning
☐ saving

5. S-T-R-E-T-C-H: Can you think of other jobs that help keep people healthy and safe? Tell about them.

How the Wheel Rolls

Throughout history, moving heavy objects has been a huge challenge. To build pyramids, the ancient Egyptians had to drag large stones. About 5,500 years ago, another ancient people called the Sumerians discovered a trick. The Sumerians lived in what today is Iraq. Their trick was to lift a heavy object onto two wooden logs, which could be rolled. This was better than dragging! Then the Sumerians made an important **modification** that truly solved the problem of moving heavy things. They cut a slice off the roller. Presto, now they had a wheel! This is one invention that really caught on. Thanks to the Sumerians, first there were carts, then bikes, trains, and cars.

KEY QUESTIONS

1. PROBLEM: What problem is described in this passage?

2. SOLUTION: How is it solved?

3. DETAILS: In what modern-day country was the wheel invented?

4. CONTEXT CLUES: What do you think *modification* means?

☐ change
☐ roll
☐ yell

5. S-T-R-E-T-C-H: How do you use wheels in your daily life? Tell about it.

Ending Polio

A disease called polio was once very common in the United States. It harmed thousands of people each year. It was very serious and could even be **fatal**. Some of those who had the disease were left with weak leg muscles, making it hard to walk. One of those was Franklin Roosevelt, the 32nd president of the United States. But in 1952, a scientist named Jonas Salk developed a vaccine for polio. Then in 1955, the vaccine was introduced to the world. The vaccine, given by a shot, protected people from getting the disease. Thanks to Jonas Salk, polio in the United States is mostly a thing of the past.

KEY QUESTIONS

1. PROBLEM: What problem is described in this passage?

2. SOLUTION: How is it solved?

3. TEXT EVIDENCE: What year was the vaccine introduced? Cite the text.

4. CONTEXT CLUES: What do you think *fatal* means?

☐ deadly
☐ scary
☐ uncomfortable

5. S-T-R-E-T-C-H: Why does the author say that polio is "mostly a thing of the past"?

Recycling Really Rocks!

Some types of garbage, like potato skins and apple peels, quickly rot away. Other things, such as metal, glass, and plastic, break down much more slowly. It takes about 100 years for an empty soup can to **decompose**. A plastic water bottle takes about 450 years. During that time, dangerous chemicals get released into the ground or water. Fortunately, metal, plastic, and glass can be melted down and turned into new cans and bottles. That's called recycling. Recycling really rocks!

KEY QUESTIONS

1. PROBLEM: What problem is described in this passage?

2. SOLUTION: How is it solved?

3. TEXT EVIDENCE: How long does it take an empty soup can to decompose? Cite the text.

4. CONTEXT CLUES: What do you think *decompose* means?

☐ spill
☐ explode
☐ break down

5. S-T-R-E-T-C-H: Do you think recycling is a good thing? Tell why.

The Gold Rush

In the early 1800s, not many people lived in California. It was very **sparsely** populated. Then, in 1848, a man was building a mill in California. When he looked into a stream, he noticed some tiny bits of gold. The man tried to keep his discovery secret. But news got out. Because gold had been found, people rushed into California. Over the next few years, about 300,000 people from all over the world moved there to try to strike it rich. That's how the Gold Rush helped settle the American West.

KEY QUESTIONS

1. CAUSE: What caused the Gold Rush?

2. EFFECT: What effect did the discovery of gold have on California?

3. CAUSE AND EFFECT: Complete this sentence frame: In this passage, the cause is _____, and the effect is _____.

4. CONTEXT CLUES: What do you think *sparsely* means?

- [ ] a lot
- [ ] not many
- [ ] a vegetable

5. S-T-R-E-T-C-H: Do you think it would have been fun to go to California during the Gold Rush? Why or why not?

The End of Dinosaurs

Long before humans arrived, dinosaurs ruled the planet. Some of the ancient dinosaurs weren't much bigger than humans, but others were massive, with skulls as big as a car. So what happened to these giant creatures? Why did they become extinct? Many experts think that about 65 million years ago, a giant asteroid crashed into Earth. Asteroids are huge rocks orbiting out in space. They're big enough to cause a lot of damage in a collision. According to this theory, the asteroid made Earth **uninhabitable** for dinosaurs. Under the new conditions, the mighty creatures died out.

KEY QUESTIONS

1. CAUSE: According to the theory in the passage, what caused the dinosaurs to die out?

2. EFFECT: According to the theory, what effect did the asteroid have on the dinosaurs?

3. CAUSE AND EFFECT: Complete this sentence frame: In this passage, the cause is _____, and the effect is _____.

4. CONTEXT CLUES: What do you think *uninhabitable* means?

- [ ] not familiar
- [ ] very unusual
- [ ] not fit for living

5. S-T-R-E-T-C-H: Do you think all the dinosaurs really died out? Explain.

Hare Turns White

Snowshoe hares live in mountain forests in places like Alaska and Montana. What is **extraordinary** about these rabbits is how they change color. They have brown fur during the spring and summer. But the cold winter weather makes their fur turn white! The snowshoe hare's new white coat allows this mammal to blend in with the snow. It is hard for predators to see them. What else makes these hares special? They have bigger back feet than other hares, which makes them look like they're wearing snowshoes. In fact, that's where their name comes from.

KEY QUESTIONS

1. CAUSE: What causes a snowshoe hare's fur to change color?

2. EFFECT: What effect does the winter weather have on snowshoe hares?

3. CAUSE AND EFFECT: Complete this sentence frame: In this passage, the cause is _____, and the effect is _____.

4. CONTEXT CLUES: What do you think *extraordinary* means?

☐ outstanding
☐ additional
☐ normal

5. S-T-R-E-T-C-H: The snowshoe hare has a name that fits it well. What's another well-named animal and why?

Tears and Triumph

Shah Jahan was an emperor who lived in India about 400 years ago. He deeply loved his wife, Mumtaz Mahal. When she died, Shah Jahan was heartbroken. He wanted a grand place to bury her body. So he decided to build the Taj Mahal—a massive **mausoleum**, as big as the love he had lost. It took 22 years, countless workers, and a team of 1,000 elephants to build the Taj Mahal. It is considered one of the great wonders of the world. Every year, the site is visited by about four million tourists. Maybe you can see it one day!

KEY QUESTIONS

1. CAUSE: What caused the emperor to feel sad?

2. EFFECT: What effect did his sadness have?

3. CAUSE AND EFFECT: Complete this sentence frame: In this passage, the cause is _____, and the effect is _____.

4. CONTEXT CLUES: What do you think *mausoleum* means?

☐ a building with tombs
☐ a traffic signal
☐ a type of flower

5. S-T-R-E-T-C-H: Why do you think this passage is called "Tears and Triumph"?

INFO TEXT: CAUSE AND EFFECT

From Green to Red

Tomatoes are red, right? Well, that depends on when you're looking at them. Most ripe tomatoes are red, but when they're growing on the vine, they start out green. They turn red only as they become ripe. So what causes this color change? It all comes down to a chemical called lycopene. As tomatoes ripen, lycopene develops in the fruit, which creates a red **pigment**. In the early weeks, tomatoes don't have much lycopene. But as they slowly ripen, the lycopene increases. When tomatoes turn bright red, they are ready to eat. Delicious!

KEY QUESTIONS

1. CAUSE: What causes tomatoes on the vine to change color?

2. EFFECT: What effect does lycopene have on tomatoes?

3. CAUSE AND EFFECT: Complete this sentence frame: In this passage, the cause is _____, and the effect is _____.

4. CONTEXT CLUES: What do you think *pigment* means?

☐ ripe
☐ stem
☐ color

5. S-T-R-E-T-C-H: Can you think of another fruit or vegetable that changes color as it ripens? Describe how it changes.

INFO TEXT: CAUSE AND EFFECT

The Problem With Crowded Beaches

Beaches are becoming more and more crowded. This is a problem for green sea turtles. These graceful creatures swim thousands of miles each year. Mother turtles return to the same beaches where they were born to lay eggs. But when beaches are filled with people, turtles can't safely make their nests and lay eggs. This is causing the number of green sea turtles to **decline**. There are so few of them left that they are now an endangered species. It is important to keep some peaceful places on beaches where green sea turtles can make their nests.

KEY QUESTIONS

1. CAUSE: What is causing the problem with green sea turtles?

2. EFFECT: What effect do crowded beaches have on green sea turtles?

3. CAUSE AND EFFECT: Complete this sentence frame: In this passage, the cause is _____, and the effect is _____.

4. CONTEXT CLUES: What do you think *decline* means?

☐ swim quickly
☐ get angry
☐ become smaller in number

5. S-T-R-E-T-C-H: Do you agree with the author that it is important to keep places on the beach for turtles to nest? Why or why not?

Itchy, Itchy Mosquito Bites

Summertime means fun in the sun and more time spent outside. It can also mean itchy mosquito bites, which aren't very much fun at all! But here's a question: Why do mosquito bites itch? When a mosquito bites you, she **injects** a tiny bit of her saliva into your skin. But that's not what causes the itching! It's what happens next. Your body produces a substance called histamine in response to the saliva. That's what causes the itching! Fortunately, this itching usually lasts only a day or two.

KEY QUESTIONS

1. CAUSE: What causes mosquito bites to itch?

2. EFFECT: What effect does the substance histamine have?

3. CAUSE AND EFFECT: Complete this sentence frame: In this passage, the cause is _____, and the effect is _____.

4. CONTEXT CLUES: What do you think *injects* means?

☐ swallows
☐ inserts
☐ bites

5. S-T-R-E-T-C-H: The author doesn't tell you this, but only female mosquitoes bite. Did you notice a clue in the passage? Cite the text.

Keep an Eye on the Sugar!

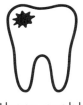 Most of us love sugar. Cakes, cookies, candy, sodas . . . there's no question that sugar is tasty. But sugar can cause problems if we eat too much of it. One of those problems is cavities in our teeth! How do those delicious goodies lead to cavities? The sugar in those tasty treats makes an acid form on our teeth. More sugar means more acid, and this acid creates tiny holes, otherwise known as cavities, in our teeth. The **bottom line** is that too much sugar leads to cavities. So remember: Don't overdo the sweets, and always brush your teeth!

KEY QUESTIONS

1. CAUSE: What causes cavities to form?

2. EFFECT: What effect does sugar have on teeth?

3. CAUSE AND EFFECT: Complete this sentence frame: In this passage, the cause is _____, and the effect is _____.

4. CONTEXT CLUES: What do you think the phrase *bottom line* means?

☐ beginning
☐ lie
☐ conclusion

5. S-T-R-E-T-C-H: Why do you think this passage is titled "Keep an Eye on the Sugar!"?

Tremor Time

The surface of Earth is not one solid piece. It is more like a puzzle with about 20 different pieces that are pushed close together. These pieces, called plates, are always moving very slowly. When one plate bumps into another, it creates **tremors**. This is an earthquake. Believe it or not, there are about 500,000 earthquakes each year! Most of these earthquakes are so tiny that people don't even feel them. But sometimes two plates bump hard, which results in a giant earthquake. A major quake can shake and damage buildings. It can crack roads and twist bridges. Fortunately, such major quakes are very, very rare.

KEY QUESTIONS

1. CAUSE: What is the cause of an earthquake?

2. EFFECT: What is the effect of bumping plates?

3. CAUSE AND EFFECT: Complete this sentence frame: In this passage, the cause is _____, and the effect is _____.

4. CONTEXT CLUES: What do you think *tremors* means?

☐ shaking movements
☐ loud sounds
☐ scary feelings

5. S-T-R-E-T-C-H: Can you think of another good title for this passage?

Your Ears in the Air

If you've ever been on an airplane, you've probably had the uncomfortable feeling of pressure in your ears. They suddenly feel stuffed up, and your hearing gets **muffled**. Why does this happen? Normally, the pressure inside your ear is the same as the air pressure around you. But on an airplane, the air pressure is changing—especially as the plane climbs and then lowers back down to the ground. This changing air pressure puts uncomfortable pressure on your eardrum. Usually a few big yawns are enough to make the feeling go away. Then you might even hear a pop!

KEY QUESTIONS

1. CAUSE: What causes the stuffed-up feeling in your ears when you're on a plane?

2. EFFECT: What effect does changing air pressure have on your ears?

3. CAUSE AND EFFECT: Complete this sentence frame: In this passage, the cause is _____, and the effect is _____.

4. CONTEXT CLUES: What do you think *muffled* means?

☐ quiet
☐ loud
☐ pressure

5. S-T-R-E-T-C-H: Can you think of another cause for stuffed-up ears?

INFO TEXT: FACT AND OPINION

Top Banana

Bananas are the very best fruit. First of all, they are sweet and **delectable**. They also have lots of potassium, which means they're good for you. They even come in their very own wrapper! Some people prefer bananas when the skins are turning brown, but they actually taste best when the skin is still bright yellow. Americans began eating bananas in the 1870s, and since then these fruits have grown in popularity. Most of the bananas we eat are grown on farms in Central America. They're picked when they're green, and they ripen after they're shipped. Apples and oranges are pretty boring in comparison. There's really nothing like a good banana!

KEY QUESTIONS

1. FACT: What is a fact that appears in this passage?

2. OPINION: What is an opinion that appears in this passage?

3. TEXT EVIDENCE: When do bananas ripen? Cite the text.

4. CONTEXT CLUES: What do you think *delectable* means?

☐ weird
☐ terrible
☐ delicious

5. S-T-R-E-T-C-H: In your opinion, are bananas the best fruit? Why or why not?

INFO TEXT: FACT AND OPINION

Let's Go Snurfing!

Snow skis have been around for thousands of years. The snowboard has only existed since 1965. It was invented by an American man from Michigan named Sherman Poppen. He **dubbed** his first snowboard the Snurfer. That's a cross between the words *snow* and *surfer*. I think snowboarding is way more fun than skiing. You can do better tricks on a snowboard. Plus, I think people look cooler going down a hill on a snowboard than on skis. I can't wait for winter. I'm going to grab my snowboard and do some snurfing!

KEY QUESTIONS

1. FACT: What is a fact that appears in this passage?

2. OPINION: What is an opinion that appears in this passage?

3. TEXT EVIDENCE: Have snow skis existed for a long time? Cite the text.

4. CONTEXT CLUES: What do you think *dubbed* means?

☐ named
☐ doubled
☐ yelled

5. S-T-R-E-T-C-H: What is your favorite winter sport? Why?

Harriet Tubman and the Underground Railroad

The Underground Railroad was neither underground nor a railroad. It was a series of routes used in the 1800s by enslaved Africans to escape to freedom. The Railroad led from the South into the northern states and Canada. Various "conductors" worked together to help people on their journeys. One of these conductors was Harriet Tubman. She was the bravest of them all. Before slavery was **abolished** in 1865, Tubman put herself in danger to help enslaved people get away. After escaping slavery herself, she made several trips to lead at least 70 enslaved Africans through the Railroad and to freedom. Tubman claimed, "I never ran my train off the track and I never lost a passenger."

KEY QUESTIONS

1. FACT: What is a fact that appears in this passage?

2. OPINION: What is an opinion that appears in this passage?

3. DETAILS: How many enslaved Africans did Tubman lead through the Railroad?

4. CONTEXT CLUES: What do you think *abolished* means?

☐ ended
☐ changed
☐ strengthened

5. S-T-R-E-T-C-H: In your opinion, was Harriet Tubman a hero? Why?

Amazing Firefighters

When there's a fire, most people get as far away as possible. But not firefighters. They are trained to run toward the blaze, so they can put it out. This is simply amazing. Firefighters are everyday heroes who deserve our undying gratitude. There are more than a million firefighters in the United States. Only about a third of them are professionals who work for their towns or cities. The majority of firefighters are volunteers, which means they don't even get paid for their efforts. These men and women **exemplify** true courage. Their bravery is so inspiring!

KEY QUESTIONS

1. FACT: What is a fact that appears in this passage?

2. OPINION: What is an opinion that appears in this passage?

3. TEXT EVIDENCE: Are most American firefighters paid to do this work? Cite the text.

4. CONTEXT CLUES: What do you think *exemplify* means?

☐ create
☐ show
☐ contain

5. S-T-R-E-T-C-H: In your opinion, what job requires the most bravery? Why?

Scary Spiders

It's time to learn about spiders. Spiders are one of the scariest animals on Earth. They aren't insects. Insects are six-legged creatures, such as grasshoppers and ants. Spiders have eight legs, which **categorizes** them as arachnids. Other arachnid relatives of the spider include scorpions and ticks. Most spiders spin webs. Webs are terrifying because you can walk right into one, which feels really icky. Most spiders have eight eyes. Having more than two eyes is just plain weird! There are about 40,000 different kinds of spiders. They live everywhere on the planet including Antarctica. *Eek!* Maybe I'll move to Mars.

KEY QUESTIONS

1. FACT: What is a fact that appears in this passage?

2. OPINION: What is an opinion that appears in this passage?

3. TEXT EVIDENCE: Do spiders live in Antarctica? Cite the text.

4. CONTEXT CLUES: What do you think *categorizes* means?

☐ upside down
☐ places in a group
☐ creeps

5. S-T-R-E-T-C-H: In your opinion, are spiders scary? Why or why not?

The Incredible Harry Houdini

Harry Houdini was a famous magician who performed in the early 20th century. He didn't perform the ordinary magic tricks other magicians did. Regular magic tricks are easy. Instead, Houdini was an escape artist. When people tied him up with ropes or locked him in a crate, he always found a way to break free. He was unbelievable! In the many years since his death, people have **exposed** some of his secrets. In one famous trick, apparently, the crate Houdini was trapped in wasn't actually locked. But even if his escapes weren't really magic, he was still the best entertainer of all time!

KEY QUESTIONS

1. FACT: What is a fact that appears in this passage?

2. OPINION: What is an opinion that appears in this passage?

3. INFERENCE: Why was Houdini known as an "escape artist"?

4. CONTEXT CLUES: What do you think *exposed* means?

☐ revealed
☐ hidden
☐ tricked

5. S-T-R-E-T-C-H: In your opinion, what is the best kind of entertainer? Why?

City Living Versus Country Living

Four out of five Americans live in cities. The three largest cities are New York, Los Angeles, and Chicago. But I'm here to tell you: Country living is best! Sure, New York has the bright lights of Times Square. But fireflies **illuminating** a country night are prettier. Sure, Los Angeles has movie stars. But horses are friendlier. Sure, Chicago has famous Lake Michigan. But the nearby pond is just dandy. And I don't have to take a bus to get there. In fact, I'm going to grab my fishing pole and head there now. Nothing beats fishing in the country!

KEY QUESTIONS

1. FACT: What is a fact that appears in this passage?

2. OPINION: What is an opinion that appears in this passage?

3. TEXT EVIDENCE: Do half of Americans live in cities? Cite the text.

4. CONTEXT CLUES: What do you think *illuminating* means?

☐ lighting
☐ flying
☐ fighting

5. S-T-R-E-T-C-H: Which do you prefer, the city or the country? Why?

Is There Really a Bigfoot?

Tales of Bigfoot sightings have been reported since the 1800s. But no one has ever proved the creature really exists. Believers say Bigfoot is a giant ape-like creature that lives in forests. Over the years, people have spotted gigantic footprints, which they believe belong to Bigfoot. In the 1960s, two men claimed to have actually filmed Bigfoot. Some who have seen this film say it really does show Bigfoot. But

others think the creature in the film is just a man in a gorilla costume. I think the film was a **hoax** and that Bigfoot doesn't exist. But for now, no one can say for sure.

KEY QUESTIONS

1. FACT: What is a fact that appears in this passage?

2. OPINION: What is an opinion that appears in this passage?

3. INFERENCE: Why is the creature called "Bigfoot"?

4. CONTEXT CLUES: What do you think *hoax* means?

☐ giant
☐ monster
☐ prank

5. S-T-R-E-T-C-H: In your opinion, does Bigfoot exist? Why or why not?

Flags Around the World

Flags rule! There are around 200 countries in the world, and every one of them has a flag. Some flags use many different colors. Swaziland's flag has five different colors and features a shield and spears. Some flags have only two colors, such as the Ukrainian flag, which has a blue and a yellow stripe. Most flags are rectangular in shape, but Switzerland's flag is square and Nepal's flag is shaped like two baseball **pennants**, one above the other. America's flag, with its beautiful stars and stripes, is one of the best. Sri Lanka's flag, which features a cool lion, is also totally awesome.

KEY QUESTIONS

1. FACT: What is a fact that appears in this passage?

2. OPINION: What is an opinion that appears in this passage?

3. DETAILS: What shape is Switzerland's flag?

4. CONTEXT CLUES: What do you think *pennant* means?

☐ a fancy necklace
☐ a long triangular flag
☐ to wave wildly

5. S-T-R-E-T-C-H: In your opinion, what is the coolest flag? Why?

Should You Spend All Your Time Gaming?

The average kid spends six-and-a-half hours each week playing video games. There are millions of different games for sale. I think kids are gaming too much. But I also think that video games are good as long as you don't overdo it. They're a way to spend time with friends and family. With some video games, you can learn about geography or history. You can even learn special skills, like how to design a building. In conclusion, I believe kids should play video games in **moderation**.

KEY QUESTIONS

1. FACT: What is a fact that appears in this passage?

2. OPINION: What is an opinion that appears in this passage?

3. DETAILS: How many hours a week does the average child play video games?

4. CONTEXT CLUES: What do you think *moderation* means?

☐ do super fast
☐ not excessively
☐ great skill

5. S-T-R-E-T-C-H: In your opinion, are video games good or bad? Why?

INFO TEXT: DEBATE

The School Schedule

Most kids follow a traditional school year, which includes a long summer break. But some kids go to school year-round, with several shorter breaks throughout the year. Some people think year-round schooling works much better. They say that a long summer break **undermines** learning because kids forget what they learned the year before. They also say that kids can get bored over the summer with too much free time. Those against year-round schooling argue that the schedule is bad for families, who look forward to shared summer vacations. They also say it's hard for kids to be stuck inside when the weather is warm and the sun is shining.

KEY QUESTIONS

1. PRO: What is an argument in favor of year-round schooling?

2. CON: What is an argument against it?

3. OPINION: What is your opinion?

4. CONTEXT CLUES: What do you think *undermines* means?

- ☐ prepares
- ☐ helps
- ☐ weakens

5. S-T-R-E-T-C-H: Can you think of another pro or con argument for this topic? Share it.

INFO TEXT: DEBATE

Perfect Pets?

Sugar gliders are becoming popular, but such **exotic** pets aren't for everyone. These tiny, big-eyed mammals are native to Australia. People find them adorable, plus they're friendly. Sugar gliders are so small they can be carried around in a shirt pocket. Although they can't actually fly, they can leap from a high spot and glide around your home. But they can be hard to take care of. Sugar gliders need a special diet that includes fresh fruit and live insects. Otherwise they can become sick. Also, sugar  gliders are active at night and make a barking sound. If a sugar glider is feeling restless, it might keep its owner awake.

KEY QUESTIONS

1. PRO: What is an argument in favor of keeping sugar gliders as pets?

2. CON: What is an argument against it?

3. OPINION: What is your opinion?

4. CONTEXT CLUES: What do you think *exotic* means?

- ☐ big-eyed
- ☐ very small
- ☐ not ordinary

5. S-T-R-E-T-C-H: Can you think of another pro or con argument for this topic? Share it.

Would You Like to Take a Space Flight?

Only a few years in the future, you may be able to travel into space. Many rocket companies are working to build spacecrafts for the **public**. These vehicles would allow regular people, not just astronauts, to experience the dream of space travel. Travelers would get a great view of Earth from outer space. They would also get to float around inside the spaceship and eat space food. Of course, there are serious concerns about public space travel. For one thing, flying in a rocket could be dangerous. It will also be super-expensive, as much as a million dollars for one trip.

KEY QUESTIONS

1. PRO: What is an argument in favor of space travel for regular people?

2. CON: What is an argument against it?

3. OPINION: What is your opinion?

4. CONTEXT CLUES: What do you think *public* means?

☐ kings and queens
☐ ordinary people
☐ market

5. S-T-R-E-T-C-H: Can you think of another pro or con argument for this topic? Share it.

A Penny for Your Thoughts?

In 2013, Canada officially did away with the penny. Some people think the United States should do the same thing. Those in favor of getting rid of the penny think that pennies are useless, since nothing costs a penny anymore. They also say that pennies are bad for the environment. Pennies are made **primarily** of zinc, and mining zinc causes pollution. Those against getting rid of pennies, however, say pennies do have uses. For one thing, they help charities. People donate unwanted pennies to charities, helping raise lots of money for good causes. And many people think pennies have value because they honor Abraham Lincoln.

KEY QUESTIONS

1. PRO: What is an argument in favor of getting rid of pennies?

2. CON: What is an argument against it?

3. OPINION: What is your opinion?

4. CONTEXT CLUES: What do you think *primarily* means?

☐ increasingly
☐ only
☐ mostly

5. S-T-R-E-T-C-H: Can you think of another pro or con argument for this topic? Share it.

School Uniforms, Yes or No?

More schools are requiring their students to wear uniforms. There are some clear advantages. Having a uniform can increase school pride and spirit.  It can decrease pressure to wear stylish clothes to try to fit in socially. Best of all, a school uniform saves kids the time and trouble of having to choose what to wear each day. But there are downsides. School uniforms can be more expensive than regular clothes. Also, school uniforms can create too much **conformity**. When everyone looks exactly the same, there's less chance for personal style and creativity. What do you think?

KEY QUESTIONS

1. PRO: What is an argument in favor of school uniforms?

2. CON: What is an argument against school uniforms?

3. OPINION: What is your opinion?

4. CONTEXT CLUES: What do you think *conformity* means?

- [ ] similarity
- [ ] relaxation
- [ ] light brown

5. S-T-R-E-T-C-H: What is your favorite outfit to wear to school? Describe it.

Too Many Trophies?

Participation trophies are often given to kids for playing on sports teams. This seems like a good thing, right? Not everybody thinks so. Some people believe that giving trophies to everyone on the team makes the trophies meaningless. They argue that trophies should be reserved for true excellence and high achievement. Those who favor the trophies, on the other hand, say they help boost kids' confidence. Trophies make every kid feel like a winner. They say the trophies give kids something **tangible** to show for their effort.

KEY QUESTIONS

1. PRO: What is an argument in favor of participation trophies?

2. CON: What is an argument against them?

3. OPINION: What is your opinion?

4. CONTEXT CLUES: What do you think *tangible* means?

- [ ] solid
- [ ] winning
- [ ] shiny

5. S-T-R-E-T-C-H: Can you think of another pro or con argument for this topic? Share it.

No More Cursive?

More and more, today's kids aren't being taught to write cursive. Some people say writing cursive is no longer **relevant**. With the rise of computers, few people need the skill. In addition, they point out that classroom time is limited. Time spent teaching cursive could be better spent on other subjects. Others, however, think learning cursive is important. They point out that some kids do better in school when they write by hand. They say that kids can write faster in cursive than in print, which means they will do better on big tests. And with cursive, kids can write their own awesome signature!

KEY QUESTIONS

1. PRO: What is an argument in favor of learning cursive?

2. CON: What is an argument against learning cursive?

3. OPINION: What is your opinion?

4. CONTEXT CLUES: What do you think *relevant* means?

☐ original
☐ important
☐ sloppy

5. S-T-R-E-T-C-H: Can you think of another pro or con argument for this topic? Share it.

No One at the Wheel

Self-driving cars were once considered science fiction. But now they are becoming a reality. Opinions are divided about whether or not these driverless cars are a good idea. Those in favor of them say that the **majority** of car crashes result from human error. They say self-driving cars will be safer. They also say that if people don't have to focus on driving, they will be free to do other things. But those who oppose the cars argue that their price will be much too expensive for most people to afford. They also argue that humans are better than  computers at dealing with the unexpected, like a dog suddenly running into the road. What do you think?

KEY QUESTIONS

1. PRO: What is an argument in favor of driverless cars?

2. CON: What is an argument against them?

3. OPINION: What is your opinion?

4. CONTEXT CLUES: What do you think *majority* means?

☐ most
☐ serious
☐ dangerous

5. S-T-R-E-T-C-H: Can you think of another pro or con argument for this topic? Share it.

Should You Be a Team Player?

It's fun to play sports such as baseball and soccer, but kids have to decide whether they want to be on a team. On a team, you can get lots of practice and play regular games. This can help you become really good. You can also make friends with other kids who enjoy the same sport. But being on a team can take up lots of time. There can also be pressure to play well, which can cause kids **stress**. Joining a team is a personal decision. Maybe you're a serious player, or maybe you'd rather enjoy a relaxed game in your own backyard.

KEY QUESTIONS

1. PRO: What is an argument in favor of being on a team?

2. CON: What is an argument against it?

3. OPINION: What is your opinion?

4. CONTEXT CLUES: What do you think *stress* means?

- [ ] athletic ability
- [ ] a feeling of peace
- [ ] worry from tough situations

5. S-T-R-E-T-C-H: Can you think of another pro or con argument for this topic? Share it.

Tablets Versus Textbooks

Tablets, such as the iPad, are becoming more popular. But there are still advantages to the good old textbook. One thing's for sure: tablets weigh less. Loading textbooks into a tablet can beat carrying those same books around in a backpack. Plus, tablets have all kinds of features, such as "search," that can make learning easier. Teachers can even email homework right to your tablet. That cuts down on the use of paper, which helps the environment. Then again, tablets are expensive. Tablets can also cause **distractions**. You might end up surfing the internet instead of doing homework. Worst of all, a tablet can crash. Textbooks don't crash.

KEY QUESTIONS

1. PRO: What is an argument in favor of tablets instead of textbooks?

2. CON: What is an argument against tablets?

3. OPINION: What is your opinion?

4. CONTEXT CLUES: What do you think *distractions* means?

- [ ] things that are unknown
- [ ] things that break up your focus
- [ ] things that hurt your eyes

5. S-T-R-E-T-C-H: Can you think of another pro or con argument for this topic? Share it.

The Mighty Elephant

Elephants are the world's largest land animal and can weigh up to 14,000 pounds. Their massive bodies are covered with thick, gray, wrinkled skin. The wrinkles help the elephant keep cool. Water collects in them and dries more slowly. Elephants' large ears provide another way to cool off under the bright sun. Elephants wet their ears and flap them like a fan. An elephant's most **distinctive** feature is its trunk. The long, snake-like trunk enables the elephant to smell, but it can also grab, hold, and pick things up. Some, but not all, elephants have tusks. Tusks are two gigantic teeth that continue to grow throughout the elephant's life!

KEY QUESTIONS

1. DESCRIPTION: What is an elephant's skin like?

2. DESCRIPTION: What animal is an elephant's trunk compared to?

3. DETAIL: How much can elephants weigh?

4. CONTEXT CLUES: What do you think *distinctive* means?

☐ clever
☐ smelly
☐ special

5. S-T-R-E-T-C-H: Briefly describe your favorite animal.

Interesting Abe

Every U.S. president is one of a kind. But Abraham Lincoln was a **rarity** even among presidents. He was the tallest president ever. He stood six-foot, four-inches. And that's without his favorite black hat, which was shaped like a stove pipe. Lincoln had a very interesting face. People who knew him noticed that he might quickly switch from a big happy smile to a mischievous grin to a look of great sadness. He also had a bushy beard. A little girl wrote him a letter telling him that's how presidents should look. He took her advice and grew his famous whiskers.

KEY QUESTIONS

1. DESCRIPTION: What does the author compare Lincoln's hat to?

2. DESCRIPTION: How would Lincoln's face change?

3. TEXT EVIDENCE: Did Lincoln have a beard? Cite the text.

4. CONTEXT CLUES: What do you think *rarity* means?

☐ unique
☐ usual
☐ young

5. S-T-R-E-T-C-H: Briefly describe how your favorite TV or movie star looks.

Maine Coons: Gentle Giants

Maine coons are the largest breed of **domesticated** cat. While the average pet cat weighs between eight and 10 pounds, Maine coons weigh up to 18 pounds and measure three feet long. The longest Maine coon ever measured was four and half feet! Maine coons have long, silky hair and come in many different colors, including white, red, silver, and mixed colors. They have bushy, raccoon-like tails that are as long as their bodies. Maine coons also have the longest whiskers of any domesticated cat, on average measuring six inches. They are sweet, intelligent, and affectionate, and for that reason, they make great pets.

KEY QUESTIONS

1. DESCRIPTION: How does the author describe this cat's tail?

2. DESCRIPTION: How does the author describe this cat's personality?

3. DETAIL: How long are a Maine coon's whiskers?

4. CONTEXT CLUES: What do you think *domesticated* means?

☐ tamed
☐ fluffy
☐ large

5. S-T-R-E-T-C-H: Describe another house cat or other pet in detail.

Powerful Tornadoes

A tornado is a powerful windstorm shaped like an elephant's trunk. As it spins like a top, a tornado picks up dirt and **debris**, making it dark in color. Tornadoes can lift heavy objects. They can move a car hundreds of feet! A tornado can yank an entire tree out of the ground, like it's pulling a weed. Tornadoes do their damage in very unpredictable ways. They move along the ground for a while, creating a path of destruction, before rising back into the air. The only thing certain about them is that they are very dangerous.

KEY QUESTIONS

1. DESCRIPTION: What animal part is a tornado's shape compared to?

2. DESCRIPTION: What toy is a tornado's movement compared to?

3. TEXT EVIDENCE: How far can a tornado move a car? Cite the text.

4. CONTEXT CLUES: What do you think *debris* means?

☐ fresh vegetables
☐ thick mud
☐ broken pieces

5. S-T-R-E-T-C-H: Describe a rainstorm in detail.

Great White Sharks

Great white sharks are the ocean's largest **predatory** fish. Because of their size (up to 20 feet long) and sharp teeth, they can be particularly deadly. Great whites are fast swimmers and can sneak up on their prey. They swim along the water's surface and as deep as 4,000 feet beneath the sea. Great whites are actually mostly gray, but their bellies are white, which is how they got their name. A great white has several rows of sharp triangular teeth. The teeth are large and serrated, which means they're jagged like the edge of a saw.

And great whites have hundreds of them. *Yikes!*

KEY QUESTIONS

1. DESCRIPTION: What color are great white sharks?

2. DESCRIPTION: What do you know about a great white's teeth?

3. AUTHOR'S PURPOSE: Is the author's main purpose to inform or persuade?

4. CONTEXT CLUES: What do you think *predatory* means?

☐ hunting
☐ hungry
☐ safe

5. S-T-R-E-T-C-H: Describe another animal that lives in the ocean.

Hot, Hot, Hot!

Ghost peppers are grown in India. They can be several different colors: red, yellow, orange, or brown. Whatever the color, they are hot, hot, hot! A ghost pepper is 400 times as hot as Tabasco sauce. A tiny **sliver** of the pepper is enough to make your mouth feel like it was set on fire. Do you still want to try a ghost pepper? Well, many restaurants now offer dishes that mix in a teeny-weeny bit of ghost pepper. It's just enough to make your tongue tingle. You can order ghost pepper chicken wings, french fries, and chili. Sound tempting?

KEY QUESTIONS

1. DESCRIPTION: If you eat a bite of ghost pepper, how will your mouth feel?

2. DESCRIPTION: How will a teeny-weeny bit of ghost pepper affect your tongue?

3. TEXT EVIDENCE: Is a ghost pepper hotter than Tabasco sauce? Cite the text.

4. CONTEXT CLUES: What do you think *sliver* means?

☐ unusually spicy
☐ a small, thin piece
☐ what a snake does

5. S-T-R-E-T-C-H: Would you like to try a sliver of ghost pepper? Why or why not?

A Little Bird Told Me

When you want to know what time it is, you **typically** look at a clock. But with cuckoo clocks, a

little bird tells you the time! A cuckoo clock is shaped like a house. Most cuckoo clocks are made of wood and have a regular clock face and hands on the front. When the hour strikes, a small door opens at the top of the house, and a mechanical bird appears. The bird sings out, making a "cuckoo" sound, to tell you the time. For example, if it's three o'clock, the bird says "Cuckoo" three times. You can tell the time, even with your eyes closed!

KEY QUESTIONS

1. DESCRIPTION: What do cuckoo clocks look like?

2. DESCRIPTION: What do cuckoo clocks sound like?

3. INFERENCE: Why are the clocks called "cuckoo clocks"?

4. CONTEXT CLUES: What do you think *typically* means?

☐ eagerly
☐ usually
☐ patiently

5. S-T-R-E-T-C-H: Invent a new clock using another animal. Describe it.

Old Faithful

Old Faithful is the name of the world's most famous geyser. A geyser happens when hot rocks deep underground boil water until the water shoots up into the air. Old Faithful is in Yellowstone National Park in Wyoming. It can be counted on to erupt not just once, but **numerous** times each day. When it does, the water blasts into the air like a tall fountain. It makes a low rumble like distant thunder. Old Faithful has a special smell, too. The gases leaking from deep underground smell like rotten eggs. Would you like to see Old Faithful? Would you like to smell Old Faithful?

KEY QUESTIONS

1. DESCRIPTION: What does the author compare Old Faithful's sound to?

2. DESCRIPTION: According to the author, what does Old Faithful smell like?

3. AUTHOR'S PURPOSE: Is the author's main purpose to inform or persuade?

4. CONTEXT CLUES: What do you think *numerous* means?

☐ many
☐ few
☐ fast

5. S-T-R-E-T-C-H: Why do you think this geyser is called "Old Faithful"?

What the Heck Is a Huckleberry?

There's Huckleberry Finn and Huckleberry Hound, but what the heck is a huckleberry? Huckleberries are small, smooth, round berries that grow in the wild. Unlike blueberries and most other berries we eat, huckleberries are not grown on farms. They grow on bushes in the forest. For that reason, they're often **foraged** by bears and other animals before humans have a chance to pick them. Huckleberries are purplish-blue in color. They look like small blueberries, and their taste is similar, mostly sweet and just a little bit tart. They have slightly larger seeds than blueberries but are just as delicious.

KEY QUESTIONS

1. DESCRIPTION: What shape and size are huckleberries?

2. DESCRIPTION: How does the author describe their flavor?

3. CONTRAST: How are huckleberries different from blueberries?

4. CONTEXT CLUES: What do you think *foraged* means?

- ☐ bought
- ☐ ate
- ☐ gathered

5. S-T-R-E-T-C-H: Describe your favorite fruit in detail.

The Art of Jackson Pollock

One of the most famous American painters was Jackson Pollock, who lived during the 20th century. He was what was known as an **abstract** artist. Pollock didn't create images of people or landscapes. Instead, his paintings are filled with splashes and drips. Often they look like a fan blew paint all over a canvas. Pollock wanted to give viewers of his paintings a feeling of motion and energy. He would use many different colors. Some of his paintings are huge, covering a whole wall in an art gallery. Fans of Pollock's paintings say you can get lost in them. Would you like to see his paintings?

KEY QUESTIONS

1. DESCRIPTION: What does the author say Pollock's paintings look like?

2. DESCRIPTION: What feeling did Pollack want to give the viewers of his paintings?

3. INFERENCE: Can a person really get lost in a Pollock painting? What does the author mean?

4. CONTEXT CLUES: What do you think *abstract* means?

- ☐ based on ideas, not actual objects
- ☐ extremely messy
- ☐ based on objects and not ideas

5. S-T-R-E-T-C-H: What is your favorite painting or work of art? Describe it.

You're Never Alone

Here's a surprising fact: You are home to a **multitude** of teeny, tiny living beings called microbes. Microbes are so small that they are invisible to the eye. These microbes live on your skin and inside your body, and there are trillions of them. In fact, right now you likely have more than two pounds of microbes on and inside you! Many of these microbes live in your digestive tract and help you digest the food you eat. Your body depends on these friendly microbes for all kinds of things, and you couldn't live without them.

KEY QUESTIONS

1. AUTHOR'S PURPOSE: Is the author's main purpose to inform or persuade?

2. MAIN IDEA: What is the main idea of this passage?

3. DETAILS: About how much do the microbes on and inside you weigh altogether?

4. CONTEXT CLUES: What do you think *multitude* means?

☐ a great many
☐ group
☐ species

5. S-T-R-E-T-C-H: Why do you think this passage is titled "You're Never Alone"?

We Need Bees!

Some people think that bees are annoying little insects that buzz and sting. But I'm here to tell you that bees are very important. They help plants grow. When bees land on plants and flowers, they get covered in dusty pollen. Then bees fly around spreading the pollen, which helps plants and flowers to multiply. Bees also **produce** things that are used by people. Of course, bees make sweet-tasting honey. Bees also make wax that is used in candles, crayons, and face creams. Rather than being frightened of bees, we should be thankful for all the good they do in the world.

KEY QUESTIONS

1. AUTHOR'S PURPOSE: Is the author's main purpose to inform or persuade?

2. MAIN IDEA: What is the main idea of this passage?

3. TEXT EVIDENCE: Is beeswax used in light bulbs, hammers, and tinfoil? Cite the text.

4. CONTEXT CLUES: What do you think *produce* means?

☐ sting
☐ make
☐ fly

5. S-T-R-E-T-C-H: Do you feel different about bees after reading this passage? In what way?

Get Up and Go!

Are you a couch potato? If so, changing your ways will make you healthier and maybe even smarter! Exercise is important for adults and kids alike. When you're active, you become stronger and more flexible, and you build stronger bones. This helps your body **function** better. Moving around can help relieve stress, and that can put you in a better mood. And scientists have found that kids did better on tests after they had 20 minutes of exercise. Plus, exercise is fun! So, whether it's riding  bikes, playing a team sport, dancing, or doing karate, just get moving!

KEY QUESTIONS

1. AUTHOR'S PURPOSE: Is the author's purpose to inform or persuade?

2. MAIN IDEA: What is the main idea of this passage?

3. TEXT EVIDENCE: What is one benefit of exercise? Cite the text.

4. CONTEXT CLUES: What do you think *function* means?

☐ look
☐ sound
☐ work

5. S-T-R-E-T-C-H: What is your favorite way to exercise? Tell why.

Know Your Fruits and Veggies

Which foods are vegetables and which ones are fruits? This may seem like an easy question, but this topic **vexes** many people. Lots of foods that are called veggies are actually fruits. For example, did you know that tomatoes and cucumbers are fruits? But here is a simple rule to help you avoid confusion: Vegetables don't have seeds inside of them. That means lettuce, potatoes, and onions are veggies. Fruits contain seeds. That means olives, peppers, and pumpkins are fruits. So next time you see a jack-o'-lantern, remember this: It's a big piece of fruit with a face.

KEY QUESTIONS

1. AUTHOR'S PURPOSE: Is the author's purpose to inform or persuade?

2. MAIN IDEA: What is the difference between a fruit and a vegetable?

3. DETAILS: What vegetables are mentioned in this passage?

4. CONTEXT CLUES: What do you think *vexes* means?

☐ expands
☐ entertains
☐ confuses

5. S-T-R-E-T-C-H: Do you prefer fruits or vegetables? Tell why.

INFO TEXT: AUTHOR'S PURPOSE

No Texting While Driving, Anywhere!

People love to send text messages. But like all things, texting has its time and place—and driving isn't one of them. This is just common sense. Drivers simply can't have their eyes on the road and on their cell phones at the same time. When a person is driving a car, he or she should have one **priority**: safety! The number of accidents that have occurred due to texting has been soaring in recent years. For that reason, 46 states have ruled texting while driving illegal. The other four states need to do the same. No one in any state should be texting while driving—ever!

KEY QUESTIONS

1. AUTHOR'S PURPOSE: Is the author's purpose to inform or persuade?

2. FACT: List one fact from the passage.

3. OPINION: List one opinion from the passage.

4. CONTEXT CLUES: What do you think *priority* means?

☐ top concern
☐ problem
☐ question

5. S-T-R-E-T-C-H: Do you think texting should be allowed while driving? Tell why.

INFO TEXT: AUTHOR'S PURPOSE

Jewels of the Sea

A pearl is a round, pea-sized white gem that is used in different kinds of jewelry. Unlike most gems, which come from the earth, pearls come from the sea. In fact, they come from oysters, a type of shellfish. An oyster lives inside a hard, sealed shell. When a grain of sand slips inside this shell, the oyster considers the sand an **intruder**. In order to protect itself, it produces a substance that covers over the grain of sand. Over time, this substance hardens and becomes the gem we know as a beautiful pearl.

KEY QUESTIONS

1. AUTHOR'S PURPOSE: Is the author's purpose to inform or persuade?

2. DETAILS: What type of shell does an oyster live in?

3. TEXT EVIDENCE: How are pearls different from most gems? Cite the text.

4. CONTEXT CLUES: What do you think *intruder* means?

☐ gem
☐ unwelcome visitor
☐ friend

5. S-T-R-E-T-C-H: If you could have a giant pearl or a small diamond, which would you choose and why?

Awesome Antarctica

Antarctica is awesome! It is the farthest south of the seven continents. It's also huge. Antarctica is nearly twice the size of Australia. And it's cold. It holds the record for the coldest temperature ever recorded, 129 degrees below zero. *Brrrrr!* Most of Antarctica is covered in ice. In some places, it's a mile thick. Even so, Antarctica is actually **classified** as a desert. That's because it gets very little rain. Still, Antarctica has many animals, such as penguins and seals. These creatures feel right at home in this huge, ice-cold desert.

KEY QUESTIONS

1. AUTHOR'S PURPOSE: Is the author's purpose to inform or persuade?

2. TEXT EVIDENCE: Is Antarctica smaller than Australia? Cite the text.

3. DETAILS: What is the coldest temperature ever recorded?

4. CONTEXT CLUES: What do you think *classified* means?

- ☐ made respectable
- ☐ put in an icebox
- ☐ put in a category

5. S-T-R-E-T-C-H: Would you like to live in Antarctica? Why or why not?

The Best Ice Cream Flavor

A recent **survey** found that vanilla is the most popular ice cream flavor in America. Chocolate came in second, and butter pecan was third. I don't agree at all. I think vanilla is a really plain flavor. It's sooooo boring. The best ice cream flavor is obviously chocolate! Chocolate is so much richer and way more delicious. In my freezer, I have a big tub of triple dark chocolate delight. In fact, I'm going to have a bowl right now. Bye!

KEY QUESTIONS

1. AUTHOR'S PURPOSE: Is the author's purpose to inform or persuade?

2. TEXT EVIDENCE: In the survey, was butter pecan ranked second? Cite the text.

3. OPINION: Which flavor do you like better, chocolate or vanilla? Why?

4. CONTEXT CLUES: What do you think *survey* means?

- ☐ waffle cone
- ☐ a group of flavors
- ☐ a gathering of information

5. S-T-R-E-T-C-H: Come up with a wacky ice cream flavor, like triple dark chocolate delight. Tell what's in it.

The Carnivorous Venus Flytrap

Most plants rely only on air, water, and sunlight to live. Plants also take nutrients from the soil. But not the Venus flytrap. The Venus flytrap is a carnivorous plant, which means it **consumes** other animals—in this case, insects. How does a Venus flytrap catch and eat insects? Its two leaves are shaped like the two sides of a clam shell. When the leaves are spread open, they produce a sweet nectar to attract insects.

When a fly or other insect lands and begins sipping the nectar, the two leaves snap shut, trapping the insect inside. The plant's chemicals soon begin to break down and digest the insect. Dinner is served!

KEY QUESTIONS

1. AUTHOR'S PURPOSE: Is the author's purpose to inform or persuade?

2. CONTRAST: How do Venus flytraps differ from most plants?

3. TEXT EVIDENCE: Does the Venus flytrap only eat flies? Cite the text.

4. CONTEXT CLUES: What do you think *consumes* means?

- [ ] resembles
- [ ] eats
- [ ] changes

5. S-T-R-E-T-C-H: What animals are carnivorous? Make a list.

Ketchup and Mustard Sandwich

Have you ever had a ketchup and mustard sandwich? It's the best snack ever! Here's why: It's easy to make, and it's tasty. Now let me tell you how to make it. First, you take two slices of bread. You squirt ketchup on one slice and spread it around with a knife. Then you squirt mustard on the other slice and spread it around with a knife. After that, you stick the pieces of bread together to make a sandwich. Ready for the final step? Eat and enjoy it! I would never suggest having this sandwich for lunch because it's neither filling nor **nutritious**. But it IS an easy-and-super-yummy snack. Have I convinced you?

KEY QUESTIONS

1. AUTHOR'S PURPOSE: Is the author's purpose to inform, persuade, or both?

2. TEXT EVIDENCE: Does the author think you should eat this sandwich for lunch? Why? Cite the text.

3. OPINION: Would you like a ketchup and mustard sandwich? Why or why not?

4. CONTEXT CLUES: What do you think *nutritious* means?

- [ ] large
- [ ] scrumptious
- [ ] healthy

5. S-T-R-E-T-C-H: What is your favorite kind of sandwich? Describe it.

SAMPLE ANSWERS

MAIN IDEA AND DETAILS

What Can a Dog's Tail Tell You? (Card 1)

1. Dogs' tails have a lot to say.
2. Sometimes a wagging tail does mean a dog is happy, but only when the tail wags to the right. (Other answers possible.)
3. According to the passage, "A wag to the left, on the other hand, means the dog is upset or stressed out."
4. *Aggressive* means "mean."
5. Answers will vary.

Hard Work Pays Off (Card 2)

1. With hard work, you can get better at just about anything.
2. When Stephen Curry was in high school, people thought he was just an average player. (Other answers possible.)
3. Yes. According to the passage, "Even now, Curry says he's always trying to improve his game."
4. *Right off the bat* means "right away."
5. Answers will vary.

Polar Bears Out in the Cold (Card 3)

1. Polar bears are well adapted to their cold environment.
2. Underneath the fur, they have a thick layer of fat, which also serves to keep them warm. (Other answers possible.)
3. They eat only fatty animals, like seals and walruses.
4. *Repels* means "keeps away."
5. Answers will vary.

The World's Biggest Marathon (Card 4)

1. New York City's marathon is the largest in the world.
2. In 2015, nearly 50,000 runners crossed the finish line. (Other answers possible.)
3. No. According to the passage, "The New York City Marathon draws runners from all over the world."
4. *Spectators* means "watchers."
5. Answers will vary.

Beetles, Beetles, Everywhere! (Card 5)

1. There are so many beetles.
2. There are nearly 400,000 different types of these insects. (Other answers possible.)
3. Yes. According to the passage, "Some beetles are pests that eat farmers' crops."
4. *Habitats* means "homes."
5. Answers will vary.

The World's Most Popular Monument (Card 6)

1. The Eiffel Tower is the world's most popular monument.
2. The Eiffel Tower was built in 1889. (Other answers possible.)
3. A lot of visitors will not want to climb all those steps.
4. *Lofty* means "high."
5. Answers will vary.

Your Fingerprints Are Yours Alone (Card 7)

1. Everyone's fingerprints are unique.
2. Fingerprints even help police identify criminals. (Other answers possible.)
3. No. According to the text, "Even identical twins have different fingerprints!"
4. *Unique* means "special."
5. Answers will vary.

A Very Special Star (Card 8)

1. The Sun is a star.
2. The Sun is about 93 million miles away from Earth. (Other answers possible.)
3. The Sun is like other stars because it is very hot. The Sun is different because it is closest to Earth.
4. *Vastness* means "largeness."
5. The Sun is special for the Earth. It keeps the planet at just the right temperature.

A Fad Called the Hula Hoop (Card 9)

1. The hula hoop is one of the biggest fads ever.
2. In 1958, it went on sale in stores. (Other answers possible.)
3. Yes. According to the passage, "100 million hula hoops were quickly sold."
4. *Fads* means "trends."
5. Answers will vary.

Very Cool Chameleons (Card 10)

1. Chameleons are one of the most interesting creatures in the world.
2. A chameleon's tongue is twice as long as its body. (Other answers possible.)
3. The author is describing how a chameleon shoots out its tongue to grab a bug to eat.
4. *Rotate* means "move in a circle."
5. Answers will vary.

SEQUENCE OF EVENTS

Making Bread (Card 11)

1. The first step is dissolving the yeast in water and sugar.
2. You put it in a pan and pop it in the oven to bake.
3. According to the passage, "During that time, the dough rises and expands."
4. *Knead* means "pound."
5. Answers will vary.

Rihanna's Dress (Card 12)

1. The first step was taking Rihanna's measurements.
2. Next, Guo Pei picked out the fabric.
3. Guo Pei is from China.
4. *Meticulously* means "very carefully."
5. Answers will vary.

What a Life! (Card 13)

1. The first thing that happens is the adult female lays hundreds of eggs in a tree branch.
2. After nymphs fall to the ground, they burrow about a foot underground.
3. They are called 17-year cicadas because they live underground for 17 years.
4. *Burrow* means "dig down."
5. Answers will vary.

Write On! (Card 14)

1. The first step in writing fiction is brainstorming.
2. The last step is proofreading your work to make sure the grammar and spelling are perfect.
3. The main idea of this passage is: This is how to write fiction.
4. *Voilà!* means "There it is!"
5. Answers will vary.

How Bees Make Honey (Card 15)

1. It lands on a flower and drinks its nectar.
2. The honey is put into the honeycomb made of beeswax.
3. The author's purpose is to inform.
4. *Regurgitates* means "spits up."
5. Answers will vary.

Getting Behind the Wheel (Card 16)

1. First, they take a driver's education class.
2. They put in months of driving practice.
3. According to the passage, "If they fail, they can continue to practice and retake the test."
4. *Authorizes* means "allows."
5. Answers will vary.

Smoothie Time! (Card 17)

1. The first step is to put ice in a blender.
2. The last step is to drink the smoothie.
3. No. According to the passage, "There are so many choices of fruit!"
4. *Frothy* means "light and foamy."
5. Answers will vary.

Biking Through the Years (Card 18)

1. The first bike was invented in 1817 in Germany.
2. A mountain bike is the last bike mentioned in the text.
3. High-wheelers first appeared in 1870.
4. *Evolve* means "change and improve."
5. Answers will vary.

Learn to Whistle! (Card 19)

1. The first thing to do is stand in front of a mirror.
2. You wet your lips and say, "ooh."
3. "Whistle like a teakettle" is a simile.
4. *Observe* means "watch."
5. Answers will vary.

Butterfly Life Cycle (Card 20)

1. A butterfly lays an egg on a leaf.
2. The egg hatches, and a baby caterpillar emerges.
3. A butterfly's long, straw-like tongue is called a proboscis.
4. *Emerges* means "comes out."
5. Answers will vary.

SUMMARIZE

The Bay Bridge Series (Card 21)

1. In 1989, the World Series took place between San Francisco and Oakland. At the start of the third game of the series, there was a big earthquake, and the game had to be postponed.
2. It was called the Bay Bridge Series because San Francisco and Oakland are connected by the Bay Bridge.
3. Yes. According to the passage, "No one at the game was hurt, but elsewhere the earthquake caused serious damage."
4. *Jolt* means "shake."
5. Answers will vary.

Meet the Liger (Card 22)

1. If you mix together a lion and a tiger, you get a liger. Ligers are real animals and are born in zoos. They are the world's biggest cats.
2. Ligers are like tigers because they are cats with stripes. Ligers are different from tigers because they have manes.
3. According to the text, "Ligers can be more than 10 feet long and weigh 1,000 pounds."
4. *Offspring* means "children."
5. Answers will vary.

A Hero Named Frederick Douglass (Card 23)

1. Frederick Douglass was born into slavery in 1818. He learned to read, even though it was illegal for enslaved people to read. When he was 20, he escaped to freedom and began working to help end slavery.
2. He continued his lessons in secret because it was illegal for enslaved people to learn to read.
3. Douglass was born in 1818.
4. *Abolitionist* means "someone who works to end slavery."
5. Answers will vary.

For Brave Climbers Only! (Card 24)

1. Mt. Everest is the highest mountain on Earth—more than five miles high. People risk their lives to climb it. The climb is very dangerous, so they have to go slowly and use special equipment.
2. According to the text, "It's part of the Himalayan mountain range in Asia."
3. The title is "For Brave Climbers Only!" because it is extremely dangerous to climb Mt. Everest.
4. *Summit* means "the top."
5. Answers will vary.

Theodore *Who*? (Card 25)

1. The famous author Dr. Seuss was really named Theodore Geisel. Dr. Seuss was the pen name he used for his books. He wrote and illustrated many books and was one of the best-loved children's book writers ever.
2. According to the passage, "He was in his 40s when he wrote and illustrated his first book."
3. Geisel wrote 44 books in all.
4. *Pseudonym* means "secret name."
5. Answers will vary.

Extra, Extra! (Card 26)

1. Kids called "newsies" worked selling papers in the old days. They worked late and got paid little, so in 1899, they went on strike and won more pay.
2. The newsies were "powerful" because people wanted newspapers, so the kids won their strike and their pay was raised.
3. The newsies' problem was low pay. They solved it by going on strike.
4. *Slogans* means "memorable words."
5. Answers will vary.

Is There Anybody Out There? (Card 27)

1. There are more than a trillion planets. They are too far away for us to study right now, but scientists do know that some of these planets orbit a sun just like Earth does. That means they could have life, just like Earth.
2. The main idea is that there could be life on some faraway planets.
3. The passage is called "Is There Anybody Out There?" because it's about the possibility of life on other planets.
4. *Astronomers* means "scientists who study space."
5. Answers will vary.

The Importance of Sleep (Card 28)

1. Even though it seems like nothing happens when we sleep, sleep is very important. When we sleep, we are recharging our brains and repairing our cells. Getting more sleep makes us happier, healthier, and do better in school.
2. The main idea is sleep is very important.

3. Three effects of getting more sleep are being healthier, happier, and doing better in school.
4. *Hit the hay* means "go to bed."
5. Answers will vary.

The Crossroads of the World (Card 29)

1. Times Square is in New York City. It is a very busy place visited by tourists from all over the world. About a million people celebrate New Year's Eve there.
2. Yes. According to the passage, "Giant billboards light the sky."
3. Tips are placed in hats to pay the musicians and dancers.
4. *Vendors* means "people selling things."
5. Answers will vary.

The Great Jackie Robinson (Card 30)

1. Jackie Robinson was the first African American to play major league baseball. It was hard because people were prejudiced, but he was strong. He became a baseball star and a great American.
2. No. According to the passage, "He played for many years."
3. Robinson joined the Baseball Hall of Fame in 1962.
4. *Admirable* means "deserving of great respect."
5. Answers will vary but should include the idea that Jackie Robinson's talent and character changed the way people thought about him and about African Americans in baseball.

COMPARE AND CONTRAST

Basketball and Soccer (Card 31)

1. Both sports are played in a rectangular area, and the ball can go out of bounds. Both sports have nets.
2. You move the ball with your hands in basketball and your feet in soccer. A basketball team can score 100 points while a soccer game might end up in a 0-0 tie.
3. No. According to the passage, "In 1891, James Naismith invented the game of basketball."
4. *Term* means "a word that describes."
5. Answers will vary.

What's the Difference Between Tortoises and Turtles? (Card 32)

1. Both are reptiles covered in hard shells.
2. They have different habitats and eat different things. Their shells are also different.
3. Turtles and tortoises are similar, but they're different species.
4. *Dome-shaped* means "rounded."
5. No, because tortoises live on land.

The Way to Go (Card 33)

1. Both are safe and will get you where you're going.
2. Plane travel is much faster. Trains travel slowly and make lots of stops along the way.
3. Train travel is usually cheaper, and you can see the scenery.
4. *Modes* means "ways."
5. Answers will vary.

Two Ways to Make Music (Card 34)

1. They both play music.
2. Orchestras are bigger, have more types of instruments, and usually play classical music. Bands are smaller and play different kinds of music, such as rock, jazz, and salsa.
3. An orchestra would probably have violins, harps, horns, and tubas.
4. *Intently* means "carefully."
5. Answers will vary.

See Ya Later, Alligator! (Card 35)

1. They are both reptiles. They are related to dinosaurs and have lived on Earth for millions of years.
2. Their snouts are different. They are different colors. Alligators like fresh water, but crocodiles like salt water. Their teeth are different, too.
3. According to the text, "They belong to the group of reptiles called Crocodilia."
4. *Snout* means "nose and mouth."
5. Answers will vary.

Great Entertainment (Card 36)

1. Both are fun, tell great stories, and transport you to other times and other worlds.
2. Movies are filmed, so you watch the action unfold. With books, you do the imagining in your head.
3. Movies and books are different, but both are entertaining.
4. *Transport* means "carry."
5. Answers will vary.

Pass the Veggies, Please! (Card 37)

1. Both never eat meat or fish.
2. Vegans follow a more restricted diet. They avoid any foods that come from animals.
3. According to the passage, "Most vegans are motivated by a concern for animals and the environment."
4. *Restricted* means "limited."
5. Answers will vary.

Boats, Small and Big (Card 38)

1. Rowboats and cruise ships are both boats. They are both ways to travel in the water.
2. Rowboats are small and can hold only a few people. Cruise ships are big and can hold thousands of people. Rowboats use oars, but cruise ships have engines.
3. Yes. According to the passage, "A cruise ship is perfect if you want to cross an entire ocean."
4. *Propelled* means "moved."
5. Answers will vary.

Two Great States (Card 39)

1. Both have small populations. Both states get lots of snow.
2. Rhode Island is the smallest state. Alaska is the largest. Rhode Island is famous for its beaches. Alaska is famous for its wilderness.
3. No. According to the passage, "About a million people live in Rhode Island."
4. *Population* means "amount of people living in an area."
5. Answers will vary.

Email Versus Regular Mail (Card 40)

1. Both email and regular mail are ways to send things.

2. Email is really fast, but regular mail is slow. You can only send an object by regular mail.
3. Regular mail is called "snail mail" because it is slow, like a snail.
4. *Instantaneously* means "immediately."
5. Answers will vary.

PROBLEM AND SOLUTION

Jumping Heroes! (Card 41)
1. The problem is that it is hard for firefighters to reach fires in the wilderness.
2. The solution is for smokejumpers to jump out of planes.
3. According to the text, "The first time smokejumpers were used was in 1939."
4. *Extinguished* means "put out."
5. Answers will vary.

Malaria Nets Make a Big Difference (Card 42)
1. The problem is a disease called malaria, which is spread by mosquitoes.
2. The solution is nets, so people can sleep inside them and not get bitten.
3. According to the passage, "The disease is carried by mosquitoes."
4. *Transmit* means "pass along."
5. Answers will vary.

Scuba Diving (Card 43)
1. The problem is that people cannot breathe underwater.
2. The solution is the invention of scuba equipment, including the oxygen tank.
3. Yes. According to the passage, "Scuba stands for 'self-contained underwater breathing apparatus.'"
4. *Apparatus* means "equipment."
5. Goggles keep water out of people's eyes. Flippers help them swim quickly through water.

Saving the American Crocodile (Card 44)
1. The problem is that the American crocodile was becoming endangered.
2. The solution was to put crocodiles on the endangered species list so it was illegal to hunt or capture them.
3. There were only about 200 American crocodiles.
4. *Endangered* means "at risk of becoming extinct."
5. Answers will vary.

A Park in the Air (Card 45)
1. The problem is a dirty, rusty stretch of unused train track in New York City.
2. The solution was turning the track into a park.
3. No. According to the passage, "In 2009, the High Line park opened."
4. *Elevated* means "placed high."
5. The park is called the "High Line" because it's made out of an old train line and it's high up in the air.

Help! I've Got an Earworm! (Card 46)
1. The problem is having an earworm, or song stuck in your head.
2. The solution is chewing gum.
3. The two pop stars mentioned are Meghan Trainor and Bruno Mars.
4. *Exasperating* means "annoying."
5. Answers will vary.

Lifeguards to the Rescue (Card 47)
1. The problem is people drowning.
2. The solution is having lifeguards at pools and beaches.
3. Lifeguards rescue more than 100,000 people every year.
4. *Vocation* means "job."
5. Answers will vary.

How the Wheel Rolls (Card 48)
1. The problem is that it is hard to move heavy objects.
2. The solution is the wheel.
3. The wheel was invented in what is now Iraq.
4. *Modification* means "change."
5. Answers will vary.

Ending Polio (Card 49)
1. The problem is a disease called polio, which harmed lots of people.
2. The solution is Jonas Salk's vaccine, which prevents people from getting polio.
3. According to the text, "Then in 1955, the vaccine was introduced to the world."
4. *Fatal* means "deadly."
5. It's mostly a thing of the past because now people can get vaccinated, so most people will not get polio.

Recycling Really Rocks! (Card 50)
1. The problem is that it takes metal, glass, and plastic a long time to break down and they release dangerous chemicals.
2. The solution is recycling.
3. According to the passage, "It takes about 100 years for an empty soup can to decompose."
4. *Decompose* means "break down."
5. Answers will vary.

CAUSE AND EFFECT

The Gold Rush (Card 51)
1. The cause of the Gold Rush was that a man discovered gold in California.
2. The effect was that lots of people moved to California.
3. In this passage, the cause is the discovery of gold, and the effect is the Gold Rush.
4. *Sparsely* means "not many."
5. Answers will vary.

The End of Dinosaurs (Card 52)
1. According to this theory, an asteroid crashed into Earth and killed off the dinosaurs.
2. According to this theory, the asteroid made Earth uninhabitable for dinosaurs.
3. In this passage, the cause is an asteroid crashing into Earth, and the effect is that Earth became uninhabitable for dinosaurs.
4. *Uninhabitable* means "not fit for living."
5. Answers will vary.

Hare Turns White (Card 53)
1. Cold winter weather causes the snowshoe hare's fur to change color.
2. The effect is they turn white.
3. In this passage, the cause is cold winter weather, and the effect is that snowshoe hares turn white.
4. *Extraordinary* means "outstanding."
5. Answers will vary.

Tears and Triumph (Card 54)
1. The cause was that the emperor's wife died.
2. The effect was that he built the Taj Mahal.
3. In this passage, the cause is that the emperor's wife died, and the effect is that he built the Taj Mahal.
4. *Mausoleum* means "a building with tombs."
5. The emperor was sad (tears), but then he built one of the great wonders of the world (triumph).

From Green to Red (Card 55)

1. The chemical lycopene causes the tomatoes to change color.
2. Lycopene turns the tomatoes red.
3. In this passage, the cause is lycopene, and the effect is tomatoes turning red.
4. *Pigment* means "color."
5. Answers will vary.

The Problem With Crowded Beaches (Card 56)

1. Crowded beaches are causing the problem with green sea turtles.
2. The effect is that green sea turtles are now an endangered species.
3. In this passage, the cause is crowded beaches, and the effect is that green sea turtles are an endangered species.
4. *Decline* means to "become smaller in number."
5. Answers will vary.

Itchy, Itchy Mosquito Bites (Card 57)

1. The cause is that your body produces a substance called histamine.
2. The effect is that the bite feels itchy.
3. In this passage, the cause is your body produces a substance called histamine, and the effect is itching.
4. *Injects* means "inserts."
5. The author writes, "When a mosquito bites you, she injects a tiny bit of her saliva into your skin."

Keep an Eye on the Sugar! (Card 58)

1. The cause is eating sugar, which makes an acid form on teeth.
2. The effect is cavities.
3. In this passage, the cause is eating too much sugar, and the effect is cavities.
4. *Bottom line* means "conclusion."
5. It's titled "Keep an Eye on the Sugar!" because it's important to watch out and not eat too much sugar.

Tremor Time (Card 59)

1. The cause of an earthquake is two plates bumping into each other.
2. The effect is an earthquake.
3. In this passage, the cause is two bumping plates, and the effect is an earthquake.
4. *Tremors* means "shaking movements."
5. Answers will vary.

Your Ears in the Air (Card 60)

1. The cause of the stuffed-up feeling in your ears while on a plane is the changing air pressure.
2. The effect is an uncomfortable pressure on your eardrum.
3. In this passage, the cause is changing air pressure, and the effect is uncomfortable pressure on your eardrum.
4. *Muffled* means "quiet."
5. Getting a cold or swimming underwater can cause ears to get stuffed up. (Other answers possible.)

FACT AND OPINION

Top Banana (Card 61)

1. Most of the bananas we eat are grown on farms in Central America. (Other answers possible.)
2. Bananas are the very best fruit. (Other answers possible.)
3. According to the passage, "They're picked when they're green, and they ripen after they're shipped."
4. *Delectable* means "delicious."
5. Answers will vary.

Let's Go Snurfing! (Card 62)

1. The snowboard was invented by Sherman Poppen from Michigan. (Other answers possible.)
2. I think snowboarding is way more fun than skiing. (Other answers possible.)

3. Yes. According to the passage, "Snow skis have been around for thousands of years."
4. *Dubbed* means "named."
5. Answers will vary.

Harriet Tubman and the Underground Railroad (Card 63)

1. The Railroad led from the South into the northern states and Canada. (Other answers possible.)
2. She was the bravest of them all.
3. Tubman led at least 70 enslaved Africans through the Railroad.
4. *Abolished* means "ended."
5. Answers will vary.

Amazing Firefighters (Card 64)

1. There are more than a million firefighters in the United States. (Other answers possible.)
2. Their bravery is so inspiring! (Other answers possible.)
3. According to the passage, "The majority of firefighters are volunteers, which means they don't even get paid for their efforts."
4. *Exemplify* means "show."
5. Answers will vary.

Scary Spiders (Card 65)

1. There are about 40,000 different kinds of spiders. (Other answers possible.)
2. Having more than two eyes is just plain weird! (Other answers possible.)
3. Yes. According to the passage, "They live everywhere on the planet, including Antarctica."
4. *Categorizes* means "places in a group."
5. Answers will vary.

The Incredible Harry Houdini (Card 66)

1. Harry Houdini was a famous magician who performed in the early 20th century. (Other answers possible.)
2. Regular magic tricks are easy. (Other answers possible.)
3. He was known as an escape artist because he would break free when he was tied or locked up.
4. *Exposed* means "revealed."
5. Answers will vary.

City Living Versus Country Living (Card 67)

1. The three largest American cities are New York, Los Angeles, and Chicago. (Other answers possible.)
2. Country living is best! (Other answers possible.)
3. No. According to the passage, "Four out of five Americans live in cities."
4. *Illuminating* means "lighting."
5. Answers will vary.

Is There Really a Bigfoot? (Card 68)

1. Tales of Bigfoot sightings have been reported since the 1800s. (Other answers possible.)
2. I think the film was a hoax and that Bigfoot doesn't exist. (Other answers possible.)
3. It's called Bigfoot because it leaves gigantic footprints.
4. *Hoax* means "prank."
5. Answers will vary.

Flags Around the World (Card 69)

1. Swaziland's flag has five different colors and features a shield and spears. (Other answers possible.)

2. Sri Lanka's flag, which features a cool lion, is also totally awesome. (Other answers possible.)
3. Switzerland's flag is square.
4. *Pennant* means "a long triangular flag."
5. Answers will vary.

Should You Spend All Your Time Gaming? (Card 70)

1. There are millions of different video games for sale. (Other answers possible.)
2. I think kids are gaming too much. (Other answers possible.)
3. The average kid spends six-and-a-half hours a week playing video games.
4. *Moderation* means "not excessively."
5. Answers will vary.

DEBATE

The School Schedule (Card 71)

1. A long summer break undermines learning because kids forget what they learned the year before. (Other answers possible.)
2. The schedule is bad for families, who look forward to shared summer vacations. (Other answers possible.)
3. Answers will vary.
4. *Undermines* means "weakens."
5. Answers will vary.

Perfect Pets? (Card 72)

1. They're adorable and friendly. (Other answers possible.)
2. They need a special diet. (Other answers possible.)
3. Answers will vary.
4. *Exotic* means "not ordinary."
5. Answers will vary.

Would You Like to Take a Space Flight? (Card 73)

1. People would get to see the Earth from space. (Other answers possible.)
2. Flying in a rocket could be dangerous. (Other answers possible.)
3. Answers will vary.
4. *Public* means "ordinary people."
5. Answers will vary.

A Penny for Your Thoughts? (Card 74)

1. Pennies are useless, since nothing costs a penny anymore. (Other answers possible.)
2. People donate unwanted pennies to charities. (Other answers possible.)
3. Answers will vary.
4. *Primarily* means "mostly."
5. Answers will vary.

School Uniforms, Yes or No? (Card 75)

1. A uniform might increase school pride and spirit. (Other answers possible.)
2. School uniforms can make everyone look the same. (Other answers possible.)
3. Answers will vary.
4. *Conformity* means "similarity."
5. Answers will vary.

Too Many Trophies? (Card 76)

1. The trophies help boost kids' confidence. (Other answers possible.)
2. Trophies should be reserved for true excellence and high achievement. (Other answers possible.)
3. Answers will vary.
4. *Tangible* means "solid."
5. Answers will vary.

No More Cursive? (Card 77)

1. Some kids do better in school when they write by hand. (Other answers possible.)
2. With the rise of computers, few people need to know cursive. (Other answers possible.)
3. Answers will vary.
4. *Relevant* means "important."
5. Answers will vary.

No One at the Wheel (Card 78)

1. Self-driving cars will be safer. (Other answers possible.)
2. They will be much too expensive. (Other answers possible.)
3. Answers will vary.
4. *Majority* means "most."
5. Answers will vary.

Should You Be a Team Player? (Card 79)

1. You can become really good at a sport. (Other answers possible.)
2. Playing on a team can take up lots of time. (Other answers possible.)
3. Answers will vary.
4. *Stress* means "worry from tough situations."
5. Answers will vary.

Tablets Versus Textbooks (Card 80)

1. You don't have to carry around all those books. (Other answers possible.)
2. You might surf the internet instead of doing your homework. (Other answers possible.)
3. Answers will vary.
4. *Distractions* means "things that break up your focus."
5. Answers will vary.

DESCRIPTION

The Mighty Elephant (Card 81)

1. An elephant's skin is thick, gray, and wrinkled.
2. An elephant's trunk is compared to a snake.
3. They can weigh up to 14,000 pounds.
4. *Distinctive* means "special."
5. Answers will vary.

Interesting Abe (Card 82)

1. Lincoln's hat is compared to a stove pipe.
2. He would look happy, then mischievous, then sad.
3. Yes. According to the text, "He also had a bushy beard."
4. *Rarity* means "unique."
5. Answers will vary.

Maine Coons: Gentle Giants (Card 83)

1. The tail is bushy and raccoon-like and is as long as the cat's body.
2. Maine coons are sweet, intelligent, and affectionate.
3. They are, on average, six inches long.
4. *Domesticated* means "tamed."
5. Answers will vary.

Powerful Tornadoes (Card 84)

1. A tornado's shape is compared to an elephant's trunk.
2. Its movement is compared to a spinning top.
3. According to the passage, "They can move a car hundreds of feet!"
4. *Debris* means "broken pieces."
5. Answers will vary.

Great White Sharks (Card 85)

1. Great white sharks are mostly gray with a white belly.
2. The great white's teeth are large, sharp, triangular, and serrated. There are hundreds of them.
3. The author's main purpose is to inform.
4. *Predatory* means "hunting."
5. Answers will vary.

Hot, Hot, Hot! (Card 86)

1. Your mouth will feel like it was set on fire.
2. It makes your tongue tingle.
3. Yes. According to the passage, "A ghost pepper is 400 times as hot as Tabasco sauce."
4. *Sliver* means "a small, thin piece."
5. Answers will vary.

A Little Bird Told Me (Card 87)

1. Cuckoo clocks are made of wood and shaped like a house. They have a clock face and hands on the front.
2. They sound like a bird singing "cuckoo."
3. They are called "cuckoo clocks" because the bird makes a "cuckoo" sound.
4. *Typically* means "usually."
5. Answers will vary.

Old Faithful (Card 88)

1. The author says Old Faithful sounds like distant thunder.
2. The author says Old Faithful smells like rotten eggs.
3. The author's purpose is to inform.
4. *Numerous* means "many."
5. This geyser is called "Old Faithful" because it can be counted on to erupt not just once, but numerous times each day.

What the Heck Is a Huckleberry? (Card 89)

1. Huckleberries are small and round.
2. They are mostly sweet and just a little bit tart.
3. Huckleberry seeds are larger than blueberry seeds. Huckleberries grow only in the wild, but blueberries also grow on farms.
4. *Foraged* means "gathered."
5. Answers will vary.

The Art of Jackson Pollock (Card 90)

1. Pollack's paintings look like the paint was blown on the canvas by a fan.
2. Pollack wanted viewers to have a feeling of motion and energy.
3. A person can sort of get lost. I think the author means you might stare at the painting and forget about everything else around you.
4. *Abstract* means "based on ideas, not actual objects."
5. Answers will vary.

AUTHOR'S PURPOSE

You're Never Alone (Card 91)

1. The author's purpose is to inform.
2. People are home to trillions of microbes.
3. They weigh more than two pounds.
4. *Multitude* means "a great many."
5. It's titled "You're Never Alone" because we always have trillions of microbes inside and on us.

We Need Bees! (Card 92)

1. The author's purpose is to persuade.
2. Bees are very important.
3. No. According to the passage, "Bees also make wax that is used in can crayons, and face creams."

4. *Produce* means "make."
5. Answers will vary.

Get Up and Go! (Card 93)

1. The author's purpose is to persuade.
2. Exercise is important.
3. According to the passage, "Moving around can help relieve stress, and that can put you in a better mood." (Other answers possible.)
4. *Function* means "work."
5. Answers will vary.

Know Your Fruits and Veggies (Card 94)

1. The author's purpose is to inform.
2. Vegetables don't have seeds inside, but fruits do.
3. Lettuce, potatoes, and onions are the vegetables mentioned.
4. *Vexes* means "confuses."
5. Answers will vary.

No Texting While Driving, Anywhere! (Card 95)

1. The author's purpose is to persuade.
2. One fact is that 46 states have ruled texting while driving illegal. (Other answers possible.)
3. People love to send text messages. (Other answers possible.)
4. *Priority* means "top concern."
5. Answers will vary.

Jewels of the Sea (Card 96)

1. The author's purpose is to inform.
2. An oyster lives in a hard, sealed shell.
3. According to the passage, "Unlike most gems, which come from the earth, pearls come from the sea."
4. *Intruder* means "unwelcome visitor."
5. Answers will vary.

Awesome Antarctica (Card 97)

1. The author's purpose is to inform.
2. No. According to the passage, "Antarctica is nearly twice the size of Australia."
3. The coldest temperature ever recorded is 129 degrees below zero.
4. *Classified* means "put in a category."
5. Answers will vary.

The Best Ice Cream Flavor (Card 98)

1. The author's purpose is to persuade.
2. No. According to the passage, "Chocolate came in second, and butter pecan was third."
3. Answers will vary.
4. *Survey* means "a gathering of information."
5. Answers will vary.

The Carnivorous Venus Flytrap (Card 99)

1. The author's purpose is to inform.
2. Most plants aren't carnivorous.
3. No. According to the passage, "When a fly or other insect lands and begins sipping the nectar, the two leaves snap shut, trapping the insect inside."
4. *Consumes* means "eats."
5. Answers will vary.

Ketchup and Mustard Sandwich (Card 100)

1. The author's purpose is to inform and persuade.
2. No. The text says, "I would never suggest having this sandwich for lunch because it's neither filling nor nutritious."
3. Answers will vary.
4. *Nutritious* means "healthy."
5. Answers will vary.